Ancient Etruscan and Greek Vases in the Elvehjem Museum of Art

Greek Vase-Painting
Essay by Jeffrey M. Hurwit

Catalogue compiled by Patricia C. Powell

Elvehjem Museum of Art
University of Wisconsin–Madison

Cover illustration: Interior of the Attic Red-figure Kylix (Type II) by the Penthesilea Painter, ca. 455 b.c., Gift of Steimke Foundation in memory of W. H. Steimke, 1976.31

ISBN 0–932900–47-x

Patricia Powell, editor
Earl Madden, designer
University Publications, producer
Ries Graphics, Butler, WI, printer

Library of Congress Cataloging-in-Publication Data

Elvehjem Museum of Art
Ancient Etruscan and Greek Vases in the Elvehjem Museum of Art / catalgue compiled by Patricia C. Powell.
p. cm.
Includes bibliography references and index.
Contents: Greek vase-painting / essay by Jeffrey M. Hurwit.
I SBN 0-932900-47-X (pbk)
1. Vases, Greek—Catalogs. 2. Vase-painting, Greek—Catalogs. 3. Vases, Etruscan—Catalogs. 4. Vase-painting, Etruscan—Catalogs. 5. Vases—Wisconsin—Madison—catalogs. 6. Elvehjem Museum of Art—Catalogs. I. Powell, Patricia C., 1942– II. Hurwit, Jeffrey M., 1949– III. Title.

NK4623.M33 E453 2000
738.3'82'0938'07477583—dc21

99-055318

Table of Contents

FOREWORD

For a university museum dedicated to supporting the teaching of arts and humanities, ancient art is the cornerstone of its mission. At least since the Renaissance, the art of ancient Greece and Rome has been admired, studied, and emulated throughout Europe and later America. Modern study of ancient art began in the eighteenth century when the German J. J. Winckelmann distinguished between the aesthetic values inherent in Greek and Roman sculpture and architecture and classified Greek art into the periods accepted today. These ideas gave rise to a new virulent form of neoclassicism in art and literature throughout Europe and even brought about such popular interpretations of Greco-Roman antiquity as those of Josiah Wedgwood. During the nineteenth and early twentieth centuries, scholarly and popular interest in the arts of Greece and Rome was sustained through the excavations of such archaeologists as Heinrich Schliemann and Arthur Evans, through the painting and sculpture of such artists as Lawrence Alma-Tadema and Jean-Léon Gérôme, through literature of such authors as Edward Bulwer-Lytton and Robert Graves, and through the writing of such scholars as John Boardman and Michael Ventris. The latter part of the twentieth century, although much less intellectually and emotionally engaged with the ancient civilizations of Greece and Rome, has, nonetheless, seen the production of such films as *Cleopatra* and *Ben Hur* that have stirred the popular imagination and of such popular television productions and books by Michael Wood as *In Search of the Trojan War* and *In the Footsteps of Alexander*.

At the core of the Elvehjem's ancient art collection is a group of Greek, South Italian, and Etruscan vases. Although small in number, it comprises an excellent teaching resource. Students at the University of Wisconsin–Madison who regularly use the vase collection range from graduate students in art history challenged to discover a new date or attribution to undergraduates exploring the history and literature of the western world. Museum docents regularly give tours to school groups. Every schoolchild in southern Wisconsin begins the study of western art and culture in the Elvehjem's gallery of ancient art. Making more information available on the individual vases will undoubtedly benefit all of the above as well as the general visitor.

Professor Jeffrey Hurwit first came to the Elvehjem in the early 1990s for a symposium on Polykleitos that had been organized by the late professor of ancient art at the UW–Madison Warren G. Moon. Professor Hurwit returned in the spring of 1999 to examine and make notes on the vases and give a well-attended talk on his research on the Acropolis.

We are indeed grateful to him for his subsequent essay on the Elvehjem vase collection that appears in this catalogue. He is eminently qualified for the task, having received his B.A. from Brown University in Classical Languages and Literatures and his M.A. and Ph.D. from Yale University in Classical Art and Archaeology. He has taught at the University of Oregon since 1980. Among his distinguished publications are *The Art and Culture of Early Greece, 1100–480 B.C.* (Cornell 1985) and *The Athenian Acropolis: History, Mythology, and Archaeology from the Neolithic Era to the Present* (Cambridge 1999).

Recognition of the contribution of Warren Moon, who taught in the Department of Art History from 1972 to 1992, in both building the collection of Greek vases and researching and publishing them, is in order. Compilation for this book required much research both in the registrar's files and in the library, which was eagerly undertaken by editor Patricia Powell, who has a long-standing interest in the ancient world. Classics graduate student Alexandra Pappas studied the Etruscan and South Italian vases and prepared comparanda. New photographs were made as required by Greg Anderson; drawings for the vase shapes were prepared by David French.

We are most grateful to the many donors to the ancient collection listed in an appendix at the back of the book as well as to the donors who made funds available for their purchase. We wish to thank the National Endowment for the Arts and the Samuel H. Kress Foundation for providing funds to make possible this publication, fourth in the new series of handbooks of the collection begun in the 1990s.

Russell Panczenko
Director

Donors to the Ancient Vase Collection

Anonymous gift in memory of Ellis E. Jensen
Frances W. English
Mr. and Mrs. Arthur J. Frank
Eloise Gerry
Warren E. Gilson
Lucien M. Hanks
Herbert M. Howe
Bruce and Ingrid McAlpine
Jacqueline Ross
State Historical Society of Wisconsin (transfer)
Steimke Foundation in memory of W. H. Steimke
University of Wisconsin–Madison Department of Classics (transfer)

GREEK VASE-PAINTING

Jeffrey M. Hurwit, University of Oregon

It is, imagine, an evening in the spring of the year when Euthynos was *archon* (chief official) of Athens—the year we call 450/49 B.C. Athens is the leading city of Greece. Silver mines, olive oil, and commerce fuel its economy. Its coffers are full of treasure captured in a series of military victories over its old nemesis, the Persian Empire. Nominally a democracy (its only full-fledged citizens are free adult males, and they are greatly outnumbered by women and slaves), Athens has forged an empire of its own, and about 160 Greek city-states throughout the Aegean pay it tribute. Perikles (although never elected *archon* in this or any other year) is the city's dominant political figure, and his program for remaking the Acropolis—for building the Parthenon and the other marble monuments on the hill—is about to get under way.

A group of well-to-do Athenian men have gathered at the home of another for a symposium.[1] The word means "drinking-party," but in fact this symposium, like symposia held among the upper classes since at least the seventh century B.C., will be a highly structured affair full of ritual, conversation, literary discussion, and entertainment. The men lie on couches placed on a raised platform set along the walls of a square room known as the *andron* ("men's room"). It is well named, for slave girls (who served and played music for the men during the party and satisfied their sexual appetites at its end) and hired courtesans (who entertained the men with their wit as well as with their bodies) will be the only women allowed in this night. This *andron* has eleven couches (men's rooms in other houses have as few as seven or as many as fifteen), and there are two men to a couch. They recline on their left sides and eat their bread and fish with their right hands. When the solid meal is done, the tables are cleared, the floor is swept, and slaves bring in water and wine. The symposium proper—a liquid occasion—begins (Figure 1).

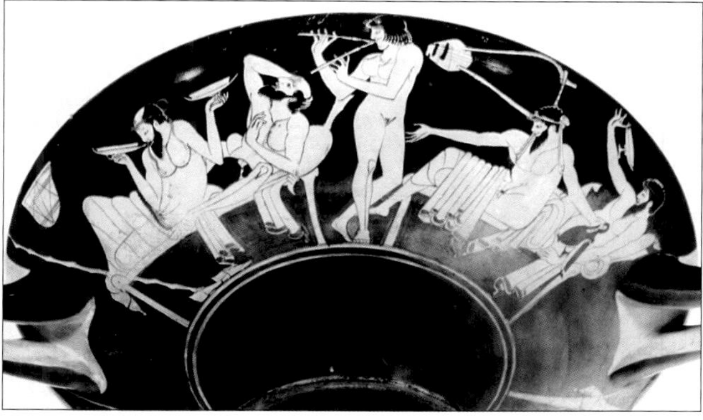

Figure 1. The symposium on exterior of a fifth-century B.C. Attic kylix. Courtesy Corpus Christi College, Cambridge, England.

The wine arrives in elegantly curved two-handled vases known as amphorai. Some wine is at once poured into a phiale (a low handleless bowl) for a shared libation, a toast drunk by the symposiasts in honor of an immortal known simply as the "Good Divinity," and to Zeus. This wine is drunk straight. But for the rest of the evening the Athenians will drink wine diluted with water (in the ancient world only the Greeks drank wine this way). The water is carried and stored in spacious three-handled vases known as hydriai, and the mixing takes place in a large, deep, wide-mouthed vase known as a krater ("mixer") set on a table in the middle of the room. The leader of the symposium determines the proportions of the mixture—five parts water to two parts wine seems to have been a popular blend, resulting in an alcoholic content close to that of many beers today—and decides that this night three kraters of wine will be drunk in all. To cool the wine a mushroom-shaped vase known as a psykter, filled with cold water or snow, is set afloat in the krater. With a dipper known as a kyathos a slave ladles the liquid into a jug known as an oinochoe ("wine-pourer") and with this proceeds to fill the cups of the men on the couches. There are several kinds of cups. Some are deep (skyphoi or kotylai, as they are known). But most are the kind of cup known as a

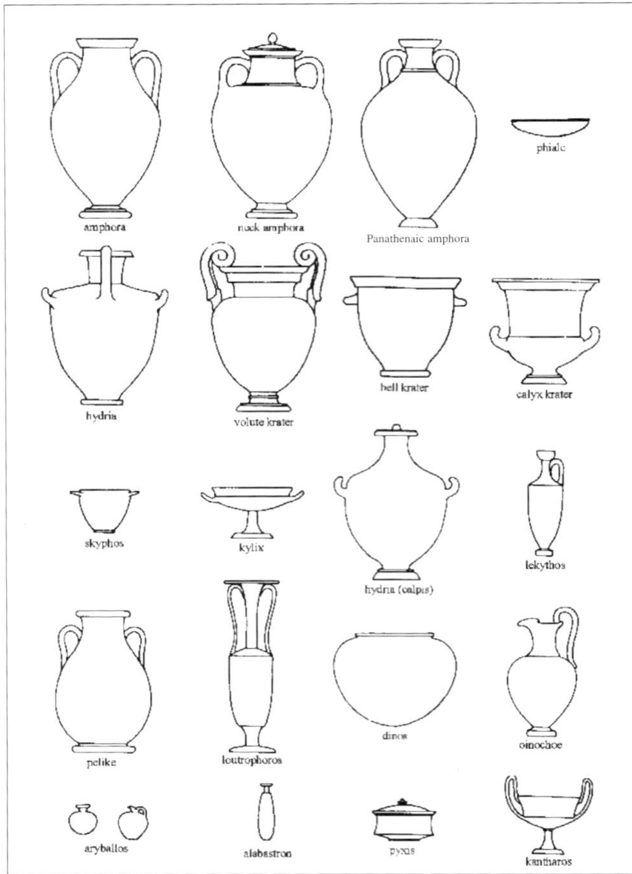

Figure 2. Diagram of Greek vase shapes.

kylix: a shallow vase with two handles set horizontally at the rim, a high stem, and a flaring foot [Figure 2].

A few of these vases are metal (bronze, silver, even gold). But most are made of clay and have been prepared, glazed, and fired in a kiln so that the terracotta is a bright red-orange and the glaze a shiny black. One man holds a kylix decorated by one of the most prolific and versatile vase-painters of early fifth-century Athens: the Penthesilea Painter [Figures 3–5; Cat. 42, 1976.31]. We do not know his real name, since (unlike some vase-painters) he never signed any of the approximately 200 vases we think he decorated. Instead, like many other anonymous vase-painters, he has had an identity and career created for him. This is done by comparing the way details such as ears or eyes or folds of drapery are rendered on different vases of roughly the same date, noting also similarities of proportion and

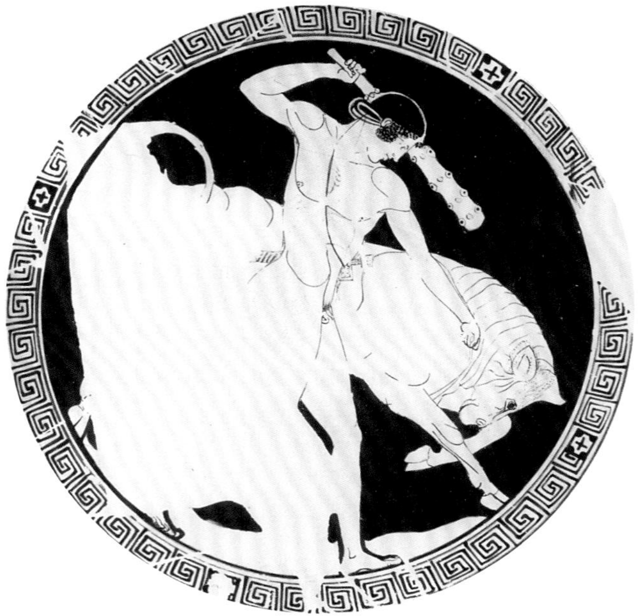

Figure 3. Interior of kylix by the Penthesilea Painter (Elvehjem 1976.31), ca. 455 B.C.

composition, and concluding that certain figures or images are close enough stylistically to have been rendered by the same "hand." The whole process is known as "attribution" and it has been going on in the field of Greek vase-painting for about a hundred years.

In the absence of a signature, the artist, once identified, is usually named after a subject on a particularly fine example of his craft (the Penthesilea Painter, for example, takes his name from a scene of Achilles slaying the Amazon queen Penthesilea on a cup in Munich), or after a city or museum where such a vase is found (for example, the Berlin Painter or the Elvehjem Painter [Cat. 19, 70.3]), or after a potter for whom the painter worked (the Amasis Painter, for example, worked for a potter named Amasis), or after a so-called "*kalos*-inscription" (the Euphiletos Painter [cf. Cat. 28, 68.14.2] is named after a youth who is praised as *kalos*, "beautiful," in words painted on an amphora in London). At all events, the attribution of particular vases to particular painters works well enough, but it is subjective business, founded upon the assumption that an artist's style, like a person's handwriting, is personal, even unique, but with the concessions that an individual style, no matter how distinctive, may evolve over the years and that, like anyone, an artist has average days and bad days as well as good ones.

The Penthesilea Painter had a pretty good day when he decorated the large kylix now in the Elvehjem. The cup is 15.3 cm (about 6 inches) tall. The bowl itself is 6.6 cm (2.6 inches) deep and is just over 37 cm (about 14.5 inches) in diameter. The result is that while this kylix could hold a lot of liquid, it could not (given the shallow curve of the rim and the nature of the human mouth) have been easy to drink from, especially by anyone reclining on his side. The diluted wine that this cup held was meant to be decorously and leisurely sipped (perhaps even shared), not drained in two or three gulps.

The cup itself was meant to be looked at: it is covered with images, inside and out. Around the exterior there are scenes of warfare: some warriors are nude, some wear cloaks, helmets, or hats, one is on horseback. Inside, in a circular field framed by a meander (or "Greek key") pattern, Theseus, the legendary king who was also the civic hero of democratic Athens, captures the mighty Bull of Marathon. Since this is the same bull that in earlier mythological time had been caught on Crete by Herakles, the greatest of all Greek heroes, and then released on the mainland, Theseus, by defeating it, reaches the same mythic level as Herakles himself (anything Herakles could do Theseus could do, if not better then at least as well). But the image does more than record a deed of Theseus and bestow Heraklean stature upon him. As our hypothetical symposiast tilts the cup and sees the image glistening through the wine, he recalls the plain of Marathon itself—the ground is just visible at Theseus' feet. This is the same ground on which, in 490 B.C., a badly outnumbered Athenian army defeated the invading Persians, a victory that a middle-aged symposiast would have remembered from his childhood and a young symposiast would have often heard about. So, Theseus' mythological victory is really a metaphor for Athens' historical victory, a victory that almost miraculously saved Athens from destruction and Athenians from servitude to *barbaroi* ("non-Greek-speakers"). Moreover, the battle on the cup's exterior (more easily seen by his couch-mate and fellow symposiasts than by the drinker himself) may represent Theseus' legendary victory over still another foe, the sons of Pallas, who challenged his rule and thus the welfare of Athens itself. Perhaps our symposiast recalls all this as he sips his wine. Perhaps, encouraged by the wine and the imagery, he passes the cup around and entertains his fellow-drinkers with the tale of Theseus and the Marathonian bull or recites some lines of poetry relating the saga. Perhaps he even recalls the Battle of Marathon and its significance for the city.

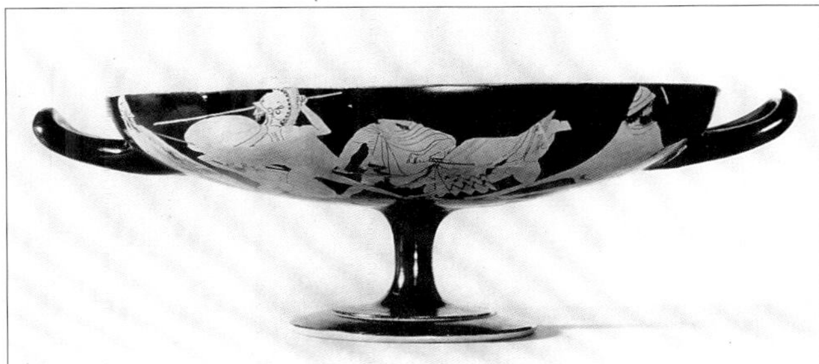

Figure 4. Kylix by the Penthesilea Painter.

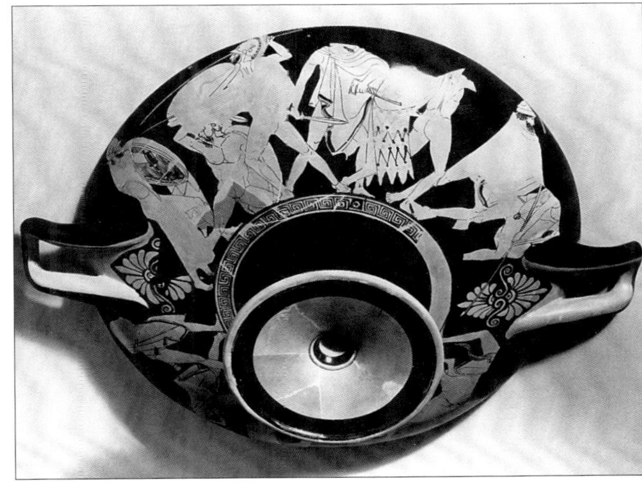

Figure 5. Exterior of kylix by the Penthesilea Painter.

This, then, is how a fine, figured vase could function at a symposium. The moderately alcoholic wine it held was meant not so much to intoxicate as to stimulate community and conversation, and the images it bore on its surfaces were meant not just to please the eye but to prompt the telling of heroic tales, the singing of poetry, and on occasion even expressions of civic pride.

When the symposium was over and the participants headed home, continuing their revels for a while in the streets (tipsy revelers are often depicted on symposiastic vases themselves, as if the images predicted the outcome of the party; cf. Cat. 22, 1979.310), the kylix was hung on the wall by one of its handles. But, remarkably, this cup's useful life did not end in an *andron* or even in Athens. Like perhaps 90 percent of all the fine, decorated Athenian vases that survive today—and it is worth noting that we have evidence for perhaps only one quarter of one percent (.0025%) of all Athenian vases ever made—the Penthesilea Painter's kylix somehow made its way to Etruria, in central Italy.[2] Whether an Etruscan tourist or middleman purchased it singly in an Athenian market for used pots and took it home with him or whether it was exported in the hold of a merchant ship carrying hundreds of vases and other more or less valuable commodities to the west, [3] the kylix ended its ancient service in an Etruscan tomb, as a gift to the dead, as equipment for a banquet meant to last for eternity.

The range of Greek vases is wide, and although the well-made and figured vases manufactured for symposia are the most familiar kinds, they were hardly the only ones. By far the most common vases were undecorated coarse wares and cooking pots and black-glazed household wares and heavy-duty transport amphorai. But there were also fine decorated vases meant for special ceremonies or rituals such as marriage or sacrifice, or for use on the athletic field or at the toilette [Cat. 18, 1978.1], or for display upon the tomb or for deposit within it [Cat. 40, 70.2].

So, too, vase-paintings present a variety of subjects. There are scenes of myth and legend and heroes—Herakles fighting the Lion of Nemea or sea-monsters or even Apollo [Cat. 22, 68.14.2; Cat. 32, 1983.6], or Ajax attacking Cassandra at the foot of Athena's statue at Troy [Cat. 30, 1985.97], or Theseus abducting Helen [Cat. 41, 69.31.1]. There are images of goddesses and gods: Artemis, for example [Cat. 37, 1985.93], but above all Dionysos, god of wine and revels, often accompanied by maenads and satyrs [Cat. 33, 1986.50]. There are so-called genre scenes representing mortals engaged in the activities of everyday life: youths with spears appealing the decision of a referee [Cat. 29, 1981.133] or conversing among themselves [Cat. 39, 1985.94], or poets singing to the music of their own instruments [Cat. 34, 1979.122], or women at home, preparing themselves with mirrors and flasks of perfumed oil [Cat. 44, 1985.98]. There are occasionally scenes where gods and mortals appear together [1.1978.2]. There are many vases simply depicting birds or mythological creatures [Cat. 24, 1983.7] or rows of animals [Cat. 17, 1983.66] or decorative patterns alone [Cat. 27, 1975.6]. Rarely, there are vase-paintings of real people or events—imagined or idealized portraits of poets like Alkaios, Sappho, or Anakreon or vaguely historical scenes of Greeks fighting Persians. There are even vases that are also sculptures, molded in the shape of animals or satyrs or human heads [Cat. 15, 1979.1117; Cat. 13, 1983.5; Cat. 14, 1979.121].

Whatever its shape, purpose, or decoration, the Greek painted vase emerged out of a tradition that can be traced back continuously to the Late Bronze (or Mycenaean) Age, when vase-painting was a "minor," even derivative art, mimicking imagery found in the finer arts of fresco or metalwork or, like the fourteenth-century cup in the Elvehjem [Cat. 1, 1979.1136], bearing such simple abstract motifs as linked spirals. In fact, for most of its history, Greek vase-painting remained a minor art. This does not mean that the Greek vase-painter could not be a skilled, even consummate draftsman. It does mean that in most periods major advances in the *way* things were represented (style) or changes in *what* was represented (subject-matter or iconography) were made elsewhere—in the art of wall- or panel-painting, for example. And there are plenty of indications that, so far as he was able (given the difficult curving surfaces of the pots he had to decorate and the limiting, highly artificial color schemes dictated by his technique), even so fine an artisan as the Penthesilea Painter attempted to imitate some of the effects of contemporary panel-painting or murals.

Still, Greek vase-painting proper begins with two impressive, basically abstract styles that stand alone as monumental achievements: the Protogeometric and Geometric styles. Probably invented in Athens around 1000 B.C., the Protogeometric style was applied above all to rounded amphorai that held the cremated remains of the dead. The style is distinguished by the use of precise, compass-drawn concentric circles and semicircles that evoke the underlying volumes of the vase: the circle (usually placed on the "belly" of the vase) suggests the full sphere of the pot, the semicircle (placed on the "shoulder" of the vase) its upper hemisphere. This is a pictureless style—or nearly so: on a handful of vases a few quickly drawn horses wander onto the otherwise abstract surface. But they are not doodles or afterthoughts. Instead, the horses probably symbolize the high status of the dead whose ashes these vases contained, "aristocrats" able to afford to own such animals.

The following Attic Geometric style (ca. 900–700 B.C.) is also basically abstract. Rectilinear patterns (such as the meander) are used to suggest the vertical and horizontal dimensions and separate parts—the architecture—of the vase, and Geometric kraters and amphorai can indeed be built large. In the eighth century, zones once filled with abstract designs are increasingly filled with genre scenes—above all funerals, processions, and battles. The masterpiece of the style is a five-foot tall amphora in Athens by the so-called Dipylon Master, placed as a marker over the grave of an Athenian woman who died around 750 B.C. [Figure 6]. The entire surface is covered with an intricate blanket of geometric patterns (and there may have been inspiration from contemporary textiles). The central zone, however, is given over to a funeral scene with stick-figure mourners gathering around the bier of the dead. These nearly identical figures, composed of circles, triangles, and straight lines, are as abstract as the human figure can be. But once it is set, as here, at the center of the vase, the human form will never really give up its place again: its inherent attraction is too strong. And so in the late eighth century more and more of the vase surface is cleared of abstract ornament and filled not only with the usual generic images of funerals, parades, and battles but also with the first Greek images that can be interpreted as illustrations of myth.

Athens was the leading center of Greek vase-painting in the eighth century, but it was not the only one. Argos, for example, was the home of another important, if very different, Geometric "school." So was Boeotia, in central Greece, and its Geometric style lasts well past 700 B.C. [cf. Cat. 10, 68.19.1]. In the seventh century even more regional styles of potting and vase-painting emerged. They are distinguished by such characteristics as the color and texture of their clays, by special shapes and techniques, or by distinctive subject-matter. So, for example, Corinth's powdery clay fires an easily recognizable pale yellow or buff (often with a greenish tinge; cf. Cat. 17, 1983.66). Some potters in the Cycladic islands specialized in large vases whose figured decoration was not painted but applied in clay relief. And East Greek vase-painters liked to cover their pots with rows of wild goats or panels of birds immersed in a variety of floating ornamental motifs (like the partridge on Cat. 11, 1979.79).

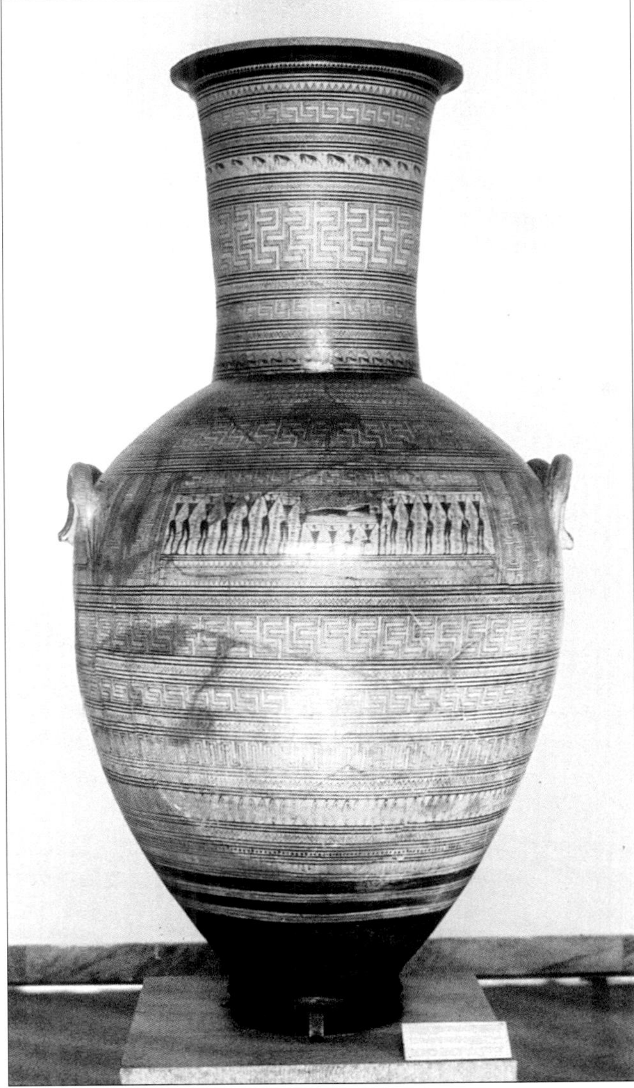

Figure 6. Amphora by the Dipylon Master, ca. 750 B.C. Courtesy National Archaeological Museum, Athens 804.

Vase-painting in the seventh century is also characterized by a wide variety of what are called "Orientalizing styles"—that is, highly ornamental styles, rich in floral motifs, curvilinear patterns, and exotic animals and monsters, influenced by the decorative repertoire of the Near East. Greece had long been in contact with such eastern

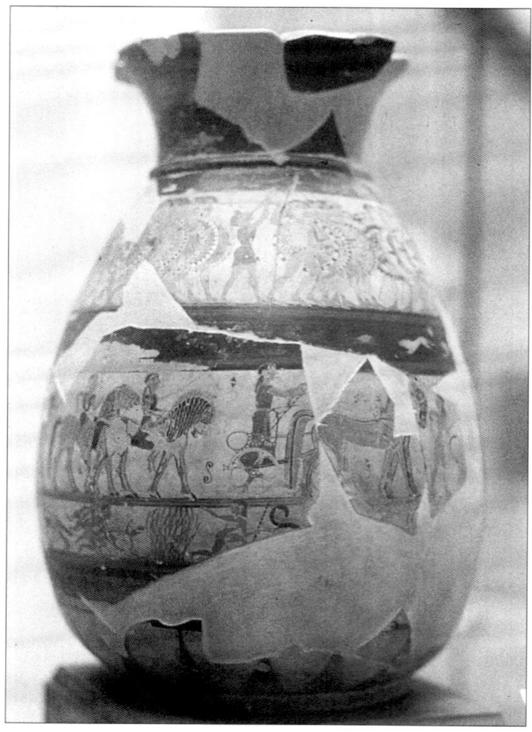

Figure 7. The Chigi vase, ca. 640 B.C.
Courtesy Museo di Villa Giulia, Rome

lands as Phoenicia and Syria: it had long imported Eastern artifacts and its craftsmen had long produced imitations or variations of Near Eastern images and patterns. But the Greek exposure to and seduction by Near Eastern styles was particularly intense from the late eighth century on.

The leading Orientalizing style was produced at Corinth and is known as Protocorinthian (ca. 720–620 B.C.). Protocorinthian potters and vase-painters specialized in small vases, especially the two-to-three-inch tall flask for perfumed oil conventionally known as the aryballos [cf. Cat. 18, 1978.1]. Their tiny, sharply curving surfaces required meticulous, miniaturist skills, and these were exercised even when the vases were a little larger. The masterpiece of the Protocorinthian style, for example, is a ten-inch tall wine-jug (or olpe) known as the Chigi Vase [Figure 7]. Made around 640 B.C. and deposited in an Etruscan tomb before the end of the seventh century, it is covered with narrow bands depicting a generic rabbit-hunt, a parade of horsemen and chariot, a double-sphinx, a lion-hunt (the lion is based on Assyrian prototypes), and an infantry battle, and the tiny figures are "polychrome" (painted in a variety of subtle browns, yellows, and reds). The only identifiable scene appears on the back of the vase where Paris, prince of Troy, judges the beauty of the goddesses Hera, Athena, and Aphrodite in the contest that will precipitate the Trojan War. But such mythological subjects are comparatively rare in Protocorinthian as a whole. More typical is the fine olpe [Cat. 17, 1983.66], made at the transition to the following Corinthian style. It is covered with four friezes filled with animals both real and imaginary (lions, frontal-faced panthers, boars, goats, deer, swans, and sphinxes), and the empty space between them is filled with patterns known as dot-rosettes. Demand for Protocorinthian and then Corinthian vases (and in particular the perfumes the aryballoi contained) was extremely high throughout the Mediterranean in the seventh and early sixth centuries, but their very popularity led to mass production and with that to the degeneration of the style. Eventually Corinthian vase-painters cashed in their meticulousness for a quicker, more careless style, stretching out their animals so that they would not have to paint quite so many of them and abandoning the precise dot-rosette for sloppier, incised blobs.

While Protocorinthian vase-painters were decorating small vases in their exacting, elegant style, Athenian potters and painters practiced a style that is very nearly its opposite: Protoattic (ca. 700–620 B.C.). It is spontaneous and dynamic where Protocorinthian is meticulous and staid, and it prefers violent mythological narratives involving heroes (Herakles, Perseus, Odysseus) and monsters (centaurs, gorgons, Cyclops) to genre scenes and repetitive parades of animals. Protoattic narratives also tend to be painted on large amphorai (tomb vases, mostly) that dwarf the standard Protocorinthian aryballos or *olpe*. Protoattic vases were meant to stay put, not travel, and the style never enjoyed the widespread popularity of Protocorinthian. Still, its concentration on mythological scenes and its monumentality are characteristically Athenian, and these traits will find grander, more careful expression at the end of the seventh century, when the style known as Attic Black Figure emerges.

It was also in the seventh century that the first great wave of Greek ceramic exports hit the shores of Etruria, and Greek vases would now, and then in the sixth and fifth centuries, reach Italy by the tens if not hundreds of thousands. While many Greek vases were acquired by the Etruscans second-hand (some, like Cat. 32, 1983.6, were even repaired in antiquity), many were also manufactured for export or were purchased new off the shelf by Etruscan agents. Some may even have been made on commission (this might explain why the Chigi vase was sealed in an Etruscan tomb so soon after its manufacture). The Etruscans, however, had their own indigenous ceramic traditions, beginning with the dark eighth-century style known as Villanovan [cf. Cat. 4, 1984.197; Cat. 3, 1979.1143]. Villanovan pots are typically handmade of "impasto" (a heavy, coarse clay loaded with stone chips and mica), and they are often incised with abstract patterns similar to those found on Geometric Greek wares (e.g. triangles and meanders). From the mid-seventh century on Etruscan workshops produced vast numbers of wheelmade vases in a more refined gray or black fabric known as bucchero [cf. Cat. 5, 1984.195; Cat. 7, 1984.196]. The surface is often highly polished and the decoration is incised or added in relief: the best bucchero tries hard to look like metal. Like the Greeks, the Etruscans also experienced a major Orientalizing movement. This is especially apparent in Etruscan metalwork, but can also be seen on such vases as the large white-on-red impasto storage jar in the Elvehjem [Cat. 9, 1978.34], made in the important city of Caere (Cerveteri) in the second half of the seventh century: the cable patterns on the lid and body and the lotus and palmette chains in the main zone are classic Orientalizing motifs. While the Etruscan Orientalizing movement was undoubtedly fuelled by direct contact with the Near East, the Etruscans were also impressed by imported Greek Orientalizing products and even try their hand at imitating the East Greek Wild Goat style, Protocorinthian, and Corinthian [cf. Cat. 20, 1978.250].

In the last quarter of the seventh century, the Protoattic style acquires greater discipline and precision and Attic Black Figure is born. Attic Black Figure is a style. But the term "black figure" properly denotes a technique: figures are black (or brown) silhouettes set against the lighter background of the clay, interior details and outlines are incised through the glaze, and added colors are used to enliven such features as drapery (reddish-purple) or women's skin (white). This highly artificial, dark-on-light color scheme is actually the result of the way the vase was fired in the kiln. Figures and patterns that were meant to be black were painted in a glaze or slip (a diluted form of the same clay used to make the vase itself). Before firing the glaze was nearly the same color as the underlying clay, and this made the acts of painting and incision difficult (unless some colored vegetable matter, burned off during firing, was added to increase visibility and contrast). The firing of the vase was a three-stage process, consisting first of an "oxidation" phase (when, with vents open and plenty of air and oxygen in the kiln, the entire vase, clay and glaze, turned light or red), then a hotter "reduction" phase (when, with vents closed and damp fuel introduced, the entire vase, deprived of oxygen, turned black and the painted areas "sintered," becoming glossy and impervious to oxygen), and finally another, cooler oxidation phase (when, with the vents reopened, the porous unglazed clay, absorbing oxygen once more, turned light or red again while the glazed figures and areas, sintered in the preceding phase, remained black).

The black-figure technique seems to have been invented around 700 at Corinth (where the use of incision may have been inspired by engraving found on imported Eastern metalwork or ivories). And vase-painters in many parts of the Greek world would adopt it (cf. the Laconian, or Spartan, cup, Cat. 27, 1975.6). But sixth-century Athenian vase-painters, blessed with an iron-rich clay that turned a vivid red-orange when fired and a glaze that turned a particularly rich, lustrous black, perfected it on vases large and small. In time, their products captured the ceramic market from Corinthian manufacturers (and in response Corinthian vase-painters even tried to imitate Attic). Early in the sixth century, it is true, there was an Attic tradition of fine miniaturist painting seen, for example, on large vases whose surfaces are divided up, à la Corinthian, into many narrow bands or friezes [cf. Cat. 23, 1985.99] or on a variety of small cups [cf. Cat. 24, 1983.7; Cat. 25, 1981.134]. But Attic Black Figure is best when it is big. Its hard outlined and incised figures seem flat, like shiny black cut-outs pasted over the red-orange clay, forming simple but often geometrically precise compositions. On the Euphiletos Painter's amphora [Cat. 28, 68.14.2], for example, the pyramidal group of Herakles and the Lion is neatly framed by the verticals of Iolaos and Athena. Herakles is the favorite Attic Black Figure action-hero, but artists such as Kleitias (ca. 570–560) and Exekias (ca. 540–530) specialize in representations of other myths (such as the Trojan War) and other heroes (such as Achilles and Ajax), while vase-painters like Lydos (ca. 560–540) and the Amasis Painter (ca. 560–525) favor scenes of Dionysos and his merry band of satyrs and maenads.

Around 525, for reasons that are not exactly clear, an Athenian vase-painter (Psiax or the Andokides Painter, perhaps) decided to turn Black Figure inside-out. He decorated a vase by leaving the figures in the red-orange color of the clay and filling the areas around them with black glaze. The experiment worked, and the new technique quickly attracted the most progressive vase-painters in the Athenian potter's quarter. In this Attic Red Figure style, interior details are rendered with a flexible paintbrush instead of a hard incising tool. Unlike incision, the painted line may vary in strength and hue (ranging from a thick black raised line to a flush line to a diluted golden brown), and this allows for a more subtle rendering of anatomy, cloth, and other details. On the Penthesilea Painter's cup [Figure 2], for example, light brown droplets are used for the knobs on Theseus's club, dark brown is used for his hair, and his stomach muscles are rendered in light yellow dilute.

The Attic Black Figure style does not end with the invention of Red Figure, and the Elvehjem boasts some fine Black Figure vases made during the first generation of the new style: the neck-amphora with Herakles wrestling Triton and trying to steal the Delphic tripod from Apollo [Cat. 32, 1983.6], for example, or the Priam Painter's hydria with Athena preparing to drive Herakles to immortality upon Mt. Olympos [Cat. 35, 68.14.1]. So, too, Black Figure would always be used for special amphorai commissioned by the Athenian state and awarded (full of olive oil) as prizes to athletic champions at its major festival, the Panathenaia. But by the end of the sixth century the leading Athenian vase-painters had recognized the advantages of Red Figure. In the fifth century, with the exception of Panathenaic amphorai, what Black Figure there is, is mostly mediocre.

One of the attractions of Red Figure was its inherent ability to mimic some of the innovations and effects of other contemporary genres, such as relief sculpture and wall- and panel-painting. For example, Red Figure is better suited for the representation of figures that seem to twist and move in space rather than stick, flat, to the vase surface. Late Archaic pioneers such as Euphronios and Euthymides (both were at their best in the years around 510 B.C.), for example, often emulate the foreshortened, space-generating or contorted figures increasingly found in marble relief and architectural sculpture. And in works by such Early Classical artists as the Niobid and Penthesilea Painters (second quarter of the fifth century), we find reflections of experiments in the representation of space and landscape ascribed in our literary sources to contemporary free painters such as Polygnotos of Thasos.

Still, the light-on-dark color scheme of Red Figure is really just as artificial as the dark-on-light scheme of Black Figure. The polychrome effects of free painting are better matched in yet another technique perfected in late Archaic and Classical Athens: White Ground, where figures are outlined in black or golden brown against a white or cream-colored background, with nonlustrous reds, blues, yellows, browns, and greens used for clothing and other details. (Another variety of white-ground is seen on an unusual cup in the Elvehjem [Cat. 34, 1979.122] with a black-figured poet singing a nonsensical song). The Penthesilea Painter painted white-ground, too. But the leading artists of the style include the Achilles and Phiale Painters (third quarter of the fifth century), who specialized in kraters and narrow flasks, or lekythoi, that, once used to anoint the dead, were deposited in or upon the grave. Typically, such white-ground lekythoi are decorated with scenes of farewell, mourning at the tomb [cf. Cat. 40, 70.2], or myths dealing with death itself.

Unlike the black-figure technique, which was practiced throughout sixth-century Greece, Red Figure is essentially an Athenian style. There are a few poor imitations on the mainland. But the only other important schools of Red Figure emerge in south Italy and Sicily in the later fifth century, apparently after the arrival of Athenian potters and painters, first as the result of colonization in the 440s and then, it seems, as a result of flight from the plague that struck Athens in 430 and from the economic dislocations of Athens' long debilitating war with Sparta (431–404). South Italian and Sicilian Red Figure is grouped into five regional schools: Lucanian (founded by the earliest known South Italian Red Figure vase-painter, the Pisticci Painter [Cat. 44, 1985.98]), Apulian, Campanian, Paestan, and Sicilian. Generally speaking, the vase shapes are essentially the same as those made in Athens. There are, however, plenty of variations and ornamental flourishes, while some schools favor certain kinds of vases and not others. So, for example, Apulian potters produced lots of volute kraters and askoi [Cat. 51, 70.18.2], while so-called fish-plates, which are also common in fourth-century Athens, are popular everywhere but Lucania [Cat. 47, 1981.132]. The subjects depicted on South Italian and Sicilian vases include plenty of mythological and genre scenes [cf. Cat. 44, 1985.98]. But there are also more idiosyncratic subjects (like female heads, depicted from the neck up, on vases such as Cat. 46, 70.18.6). And the kinds of myths depicted can also differ markedly from Athenian practice (there is an emphasis on the Underworld that is not found on contemporary Athenian vases, for example). In fact, there are some myths on South Italian vases that never appear on Attic vases (or anywhere else, for that matter). But the most striking images of all are those that appear to reproduce scenes from the tragic or comic theater (sometimes the figures wear masks and elaborate costumes or appear before stage sets).

The history of Red Figure vase-painting, both in Athens and in the west, comes to an end around 300. Pottery production, of course, does not cease, but figured vases belong now to different classes. There are, for example, a number of polychrome vases made at Centuripe in Sicily sometime in the third and second centuries B.C. that had their decoration painted in tempera pastels (magenta, lilac, pink, light blue, white, brown, and so on) *after* the pots were removed from the kiln [Cat. 63, 1976.28]. That is, the decoration is a no longer a function of the way the vase was fired, as Black and Red Figure images had always been. Centuripe vases are specialty products: they were made for rituals such as weddings and, above all, funerals. But whatever their original function and the meaning of their imagery (the faded main scene on the Elvehjem's example shows a woman visited by a winged figure or Nike), these are vases that want to be wall-paintings—in some ways they point to the style and iconography of Hellenistic and Roman murals. Their very pretensions not only remind us of the Greek vase-painter's ancient indebtedness to other, major arts but also now, toward the end of Greek art itself, indicate the exhaustion of his craft.

Notes

1. The following picture of the symposium is heavily indebted to J. Davidson, *Courtesans and Fishcakes: The Consuming Passions of Classical Athens* (New York 1998), esp. 43–52. See also O. Murray, ed., *Sympotica: A Symposium on the Symposium* (Oxford 1990).
2. For the percentages see J. M. Hemelrijk, *Schalen en scherven, een kijke in de keuken* (Amsterdam 1985), 4, and A. Johnston, "Greek Vases in the Marketplace," in T. Rasmussen and N. Spivey, *Looking at Greek Vases* (Cambridge 1991), 208.
3. In *Artful Crafts: Ancient Greek Silverware and Pottery* (Oxford 1994), M. Vickers and D. Gill argue that red-and-black Athenian vases, like Greek vases in general, were in fact exact reproductions of much more expensive vases in metal, where, for example, red-orange imitates gold and black tarnished silver. In their view, painted terracotta vases were so cheap that they had no real value and were exported virtually as ballast in the holds of ships sailing across the Mediterranean with far more expensive cargoes.

   The indebtedness of much pottery to metalwork has never been in doubt: some shapes, for example, must have originated in metal. But the notions that the vase-painter simply reproduced the designs of engravers and metalworkers (even to the point of reproducing the signatures of the metalworkers), or that the ceramic vase, just because it was inexpensive compared to gold or silver, had no intrinsic value as a work of art, are highly doubtful. See, for example, J. Boardman's review in *Classical Review* 46 (1996): 123–26, and J. J. Pollitt, in the *Times Literary Supplement* (April 14, 1995): 6–7.

Suggestions for Further Reading

J. D. Beazley, *The Development of Attic Black-Figure*, rev. ed. (Berkeley 1986).

John Boardman, *Athenian Black Figure Vases* (New York 1974).

John Boardman, *Athenian Red Figure Vases: The Archaic Period* (London 1975).

John Boardman, *Athenian Red Figure Vases: The Classical Period* (London 1989).

John Boardman, *Early Greek Vase Painting* (New York 1998).

R. M. Cook, *Greek Painted Pottery*, 3rd ed. (London 1997).

Fransçois Lissarrague, *The Aesthetics of the Greek Banquet: Images of Wine and Ritual* trans. Andrew Szegedy-Maszak (Princeton 1990).

J. V. Noble, *The Techniques of Painted Attic Pottery*, rev. ed. (London 1988).

T. Rasmussen and N. Spivey, eds, *Looking at Greek Vases* (Cambridge 1991).

M. Robertson, *The Art of Vase-Painting in Classical Athens* (Cambridge 1992).

Toby Schreiber, *Athenian Vase Construction: A Potter's Analysis* (Malibu 1999).

B. A Sparkes, *Greek Pottery: An Introduction* (Manchester 1991).

A. D. Trendall, *Red Figure Vases of South Italy and Sicily* (London 1989).

Catalogue of the Collection

Colorplates

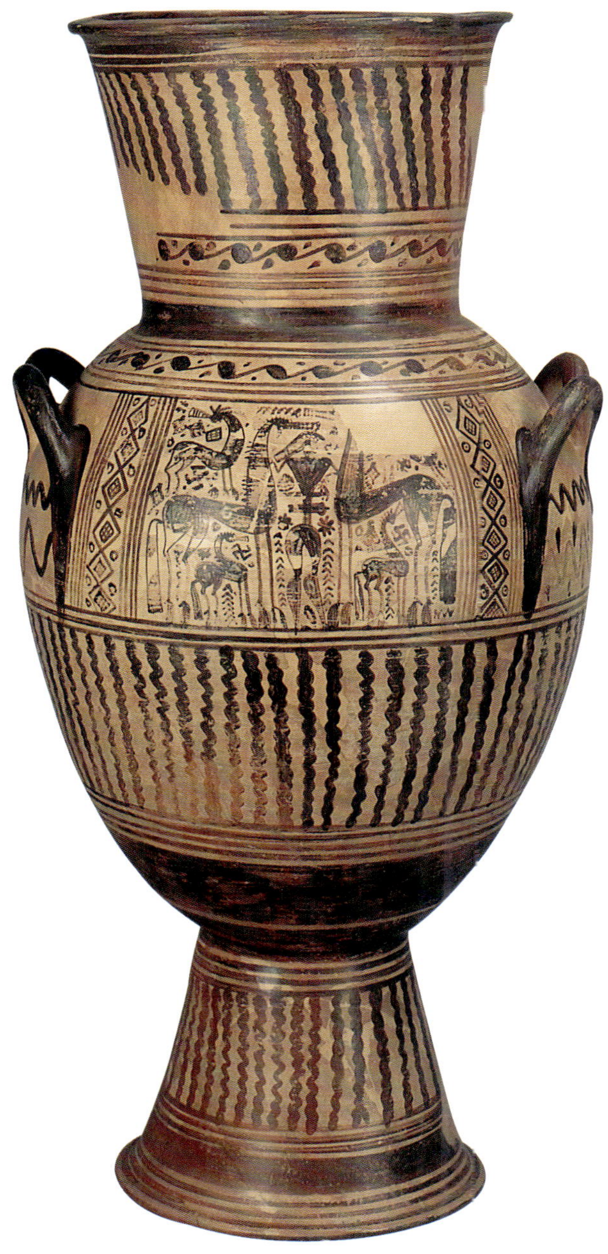

Colorplate 1 (cat. 10)
Boeotian Belly-handled Amphora (Group C)
Ca. 700–690 B.C.
H. 35 3/4 in.
Max W. Zabel Fund purchase, 68.19.1

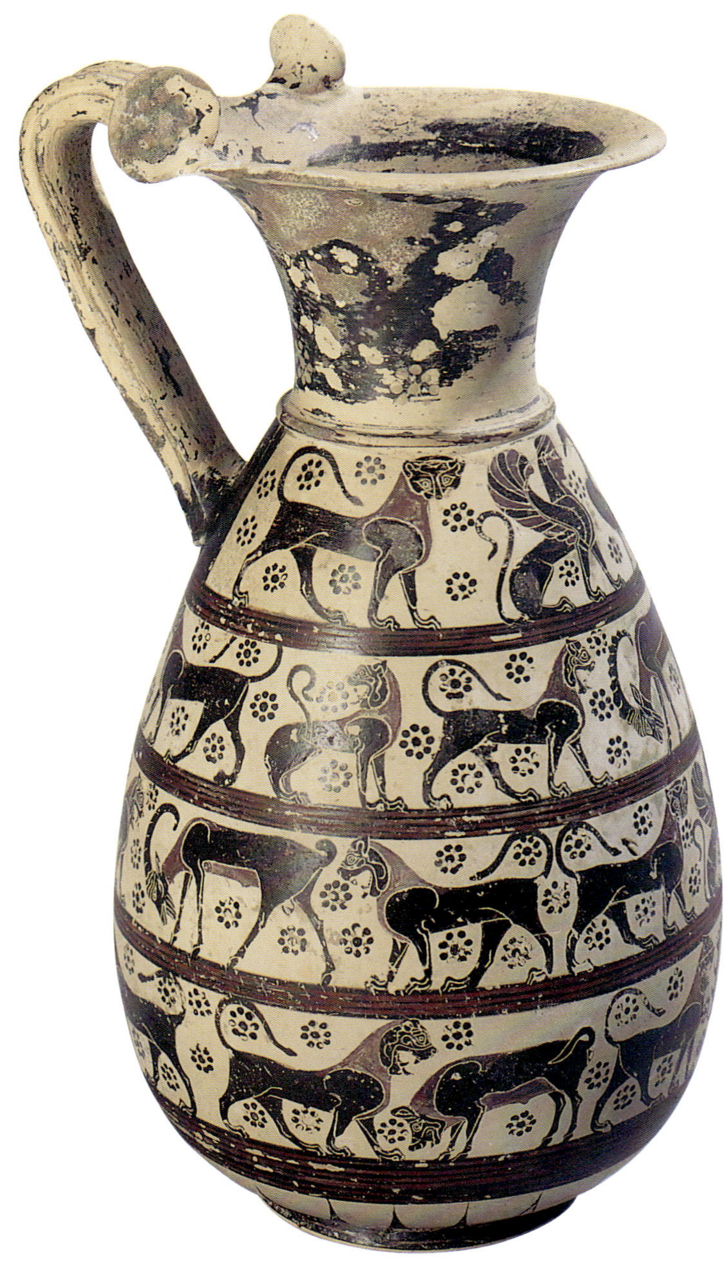

Colorplate 2 (cat. 17)
Painter of Vatican 73
Corinthian Olpe
Early transitional, ca. 640–620 B.C.
H. 12 11/16 in.
Gift of Mr. and Mrs. Arthur J. Frank, 1983.66

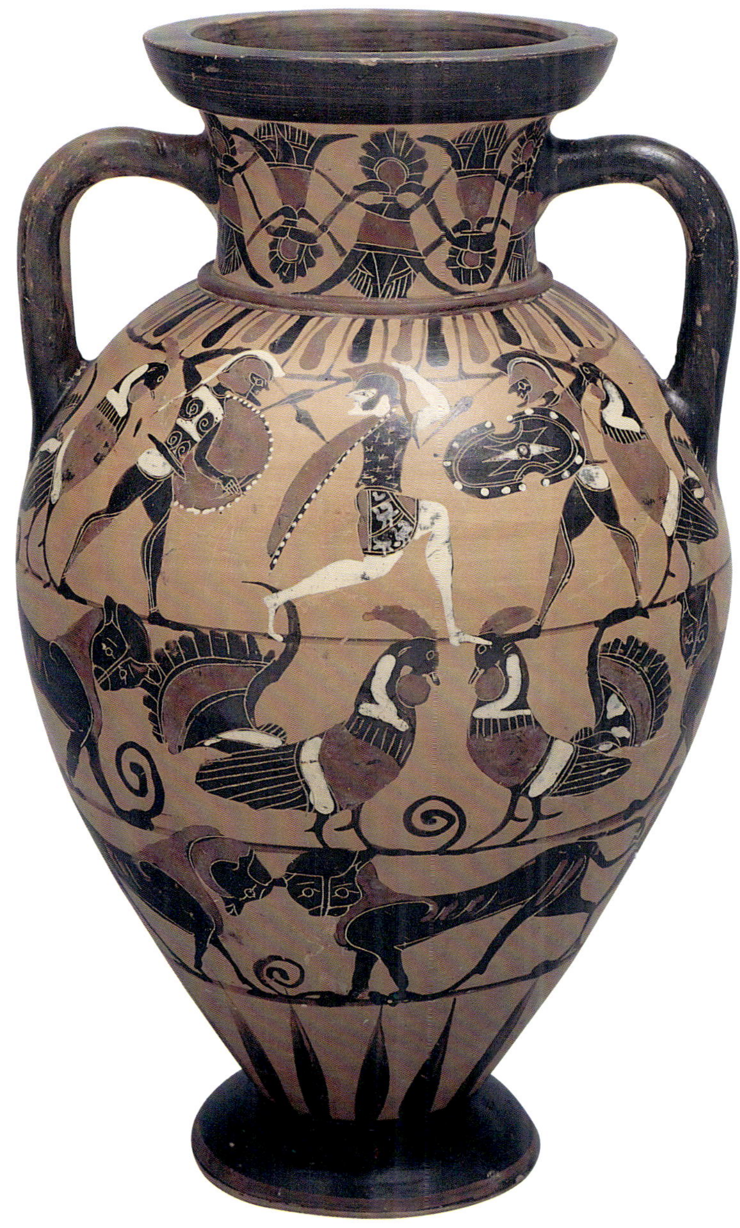

Colorplate 3 (cat. 23)
Goltyr Painter
Attic |Tyrrhenian group| Black-f.gure Neck Amphora
Ca. 565–550 E.C.
H. 15 1/2 in.
Gift of Mr. and Mrs. Arthur J. Frank, 1985.99

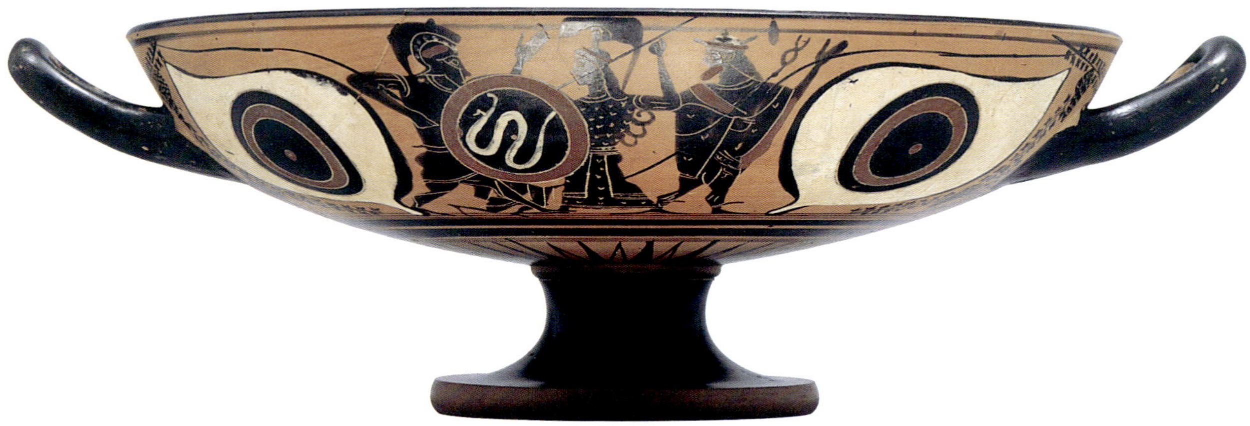

Colorplate 4 (cat. 30)
Attic Black-figure Eye-Cup
Ca. 520 B.C.
H. 4 3/8 in.
Gift of Mr. and Mrs. Arthur J. Frank, 1985.97

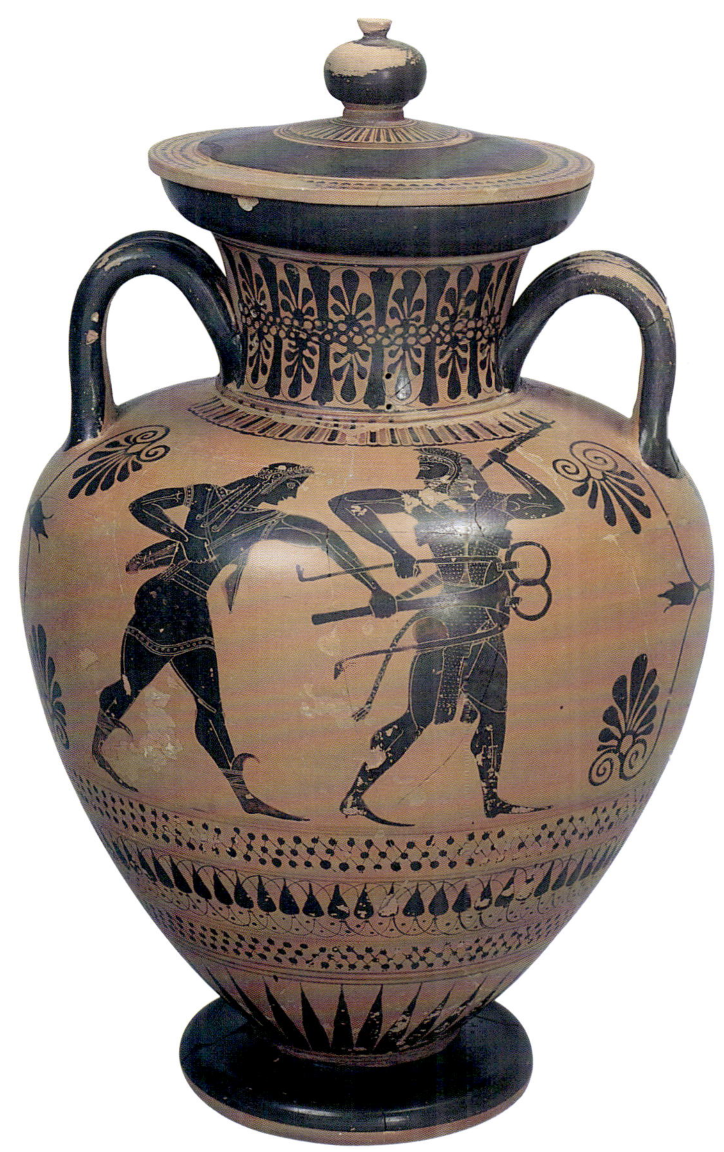

Colorplate 5 (cat. 32)
Possibly Chiusi Painter
Attic Black-figure Neck-amphora
Ca. 520–500 B.C.
H. with lid 20 9/16 in.
Tenth Anniversary Fund, Elvehjem Endowment Fund, and Art Collections Fund purchase, 1983.6

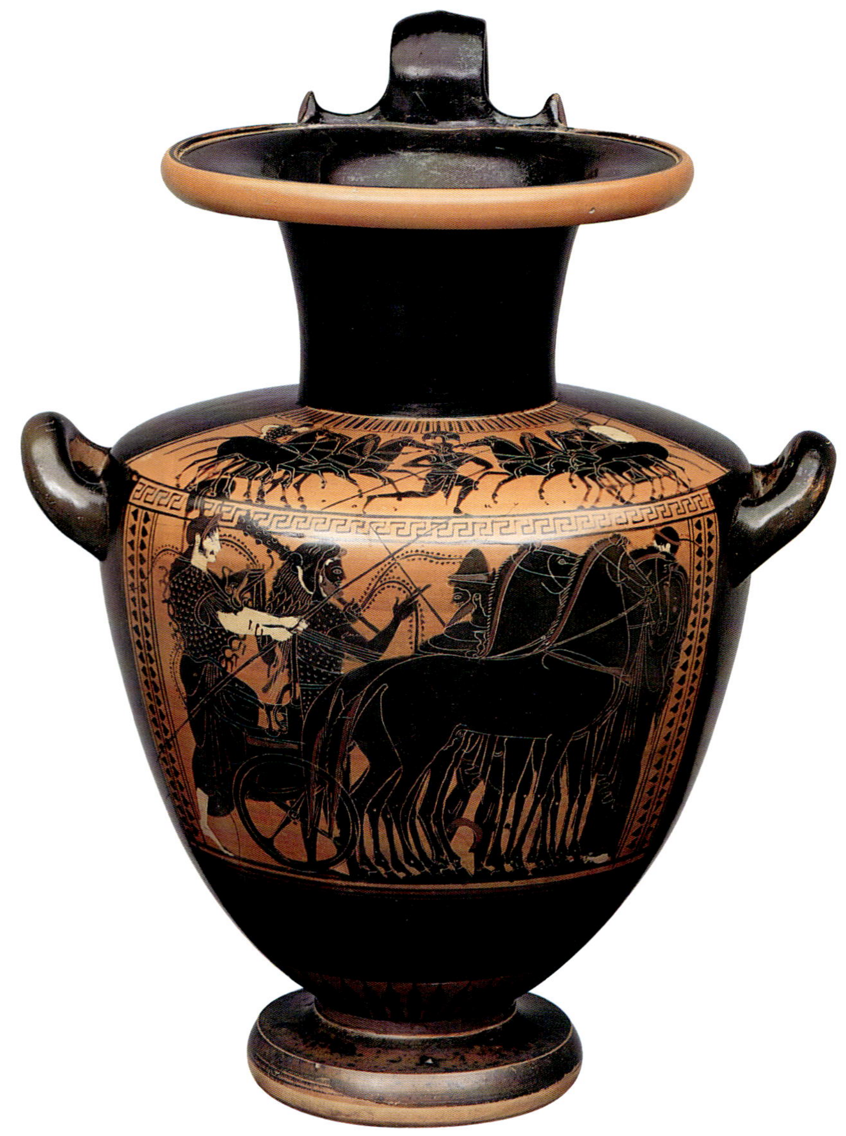

Colorplate 6 (cat. 35)
Priam Painter, Potter of the Heavy Hydrai, late 6th century B.C.
Attic Black-figure Hydria
Ca. 510 B.C.
H. 21 1/4 in.
Gift of Mr. and Mrs. Arthur J. Frank, 68.14.1

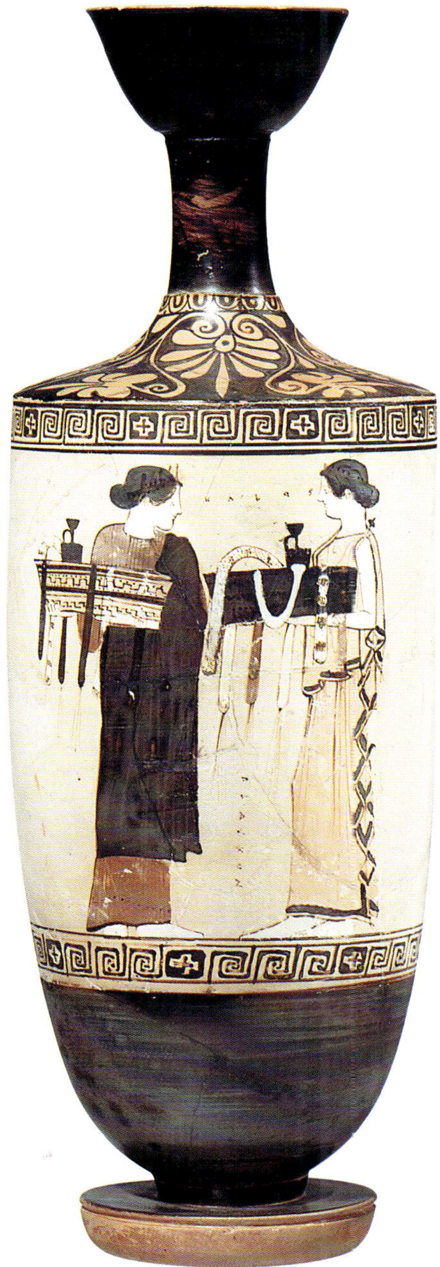

Colorplate 7 (cat. 40)
Near the Timokrates Painter
Attic White-ground Lekythos
Ca. 460 B.C.
H. 15 7/8 in.
Edna G. Dyar Fund and Fairchild Foundation Fund purchase, 70.2

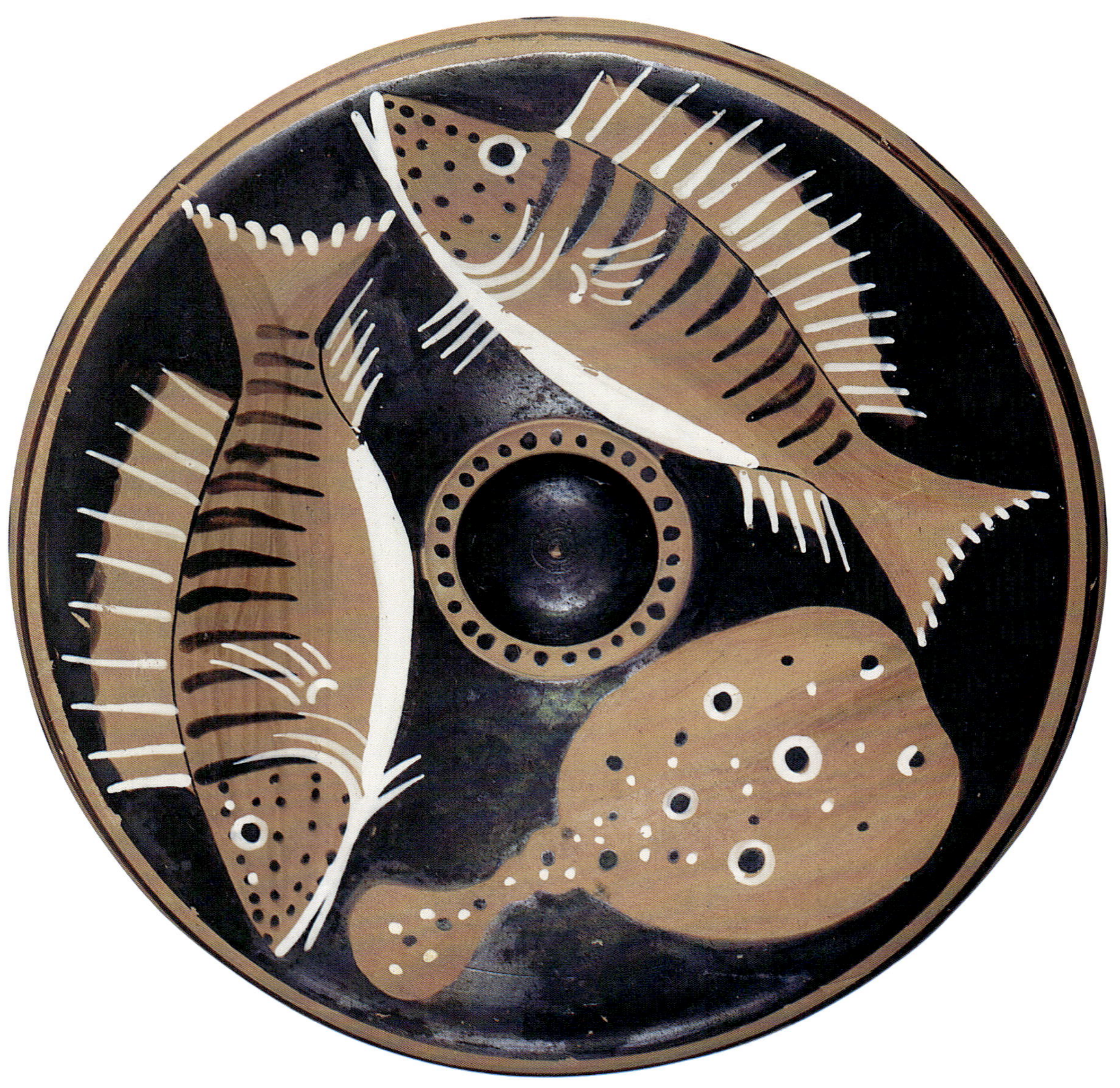

Colorplate 8 (cat. 47)
Torpedo Group
Campanian Red-figure Fish Plate
Last half of 4th century B.C.
D. 7 1/2 in.
Gift of Mr. and Mrs. Arthur J. Frank, 1981.132

1

Mycenaean Cup
Ca.14th century B.C. (LHIIIA)
H. 2 3/8 in. 6 cm; d. without handles 3 15/16 in. 10 cm; d. with handles 5 7/8 in. 14.9 cm; d. foot 1 1/4 in. 3.2 cm
Gift of Herbert M. Howe, 1979.1136, K. Adam, Athens, Greece, 1936

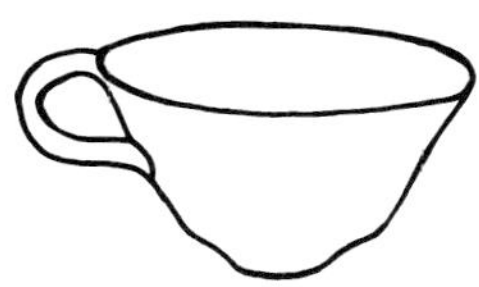

Condition: Intact. Much of paint around handle and rim has cracked and flaked. No repainting. Extensive scratches and chipping on surface throughout. Side B displays a chalky white debris that obscures painted motifs. Shallow gouge displays same pigment as paint.

Decoration: In brushed reddish natural pigment on pale buff ground are connected reverse spirals, band at lip and bottom of side, and four concentric bands on foot.

Unpublished. Cf. CVA British Museum 1 (Great Britain 1), Mycenian Pottery of Cyprus, pl. 5. no. 6. For similar shape, see A. Fairbanks, *Catalogue of Greek and Etruscan Vases* (Cambridge, Mass. 1928), pl. 5. no. 51.

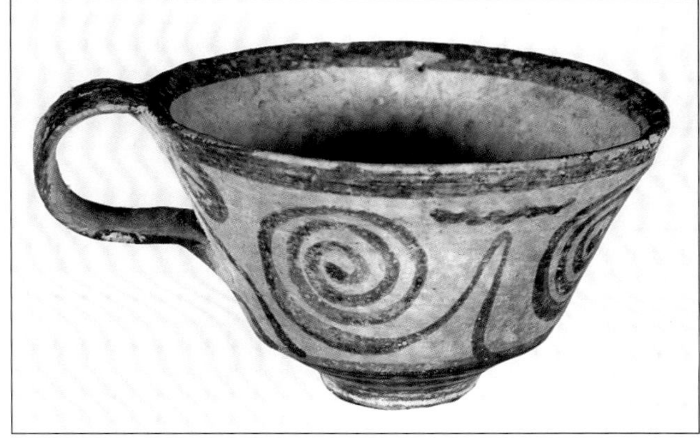

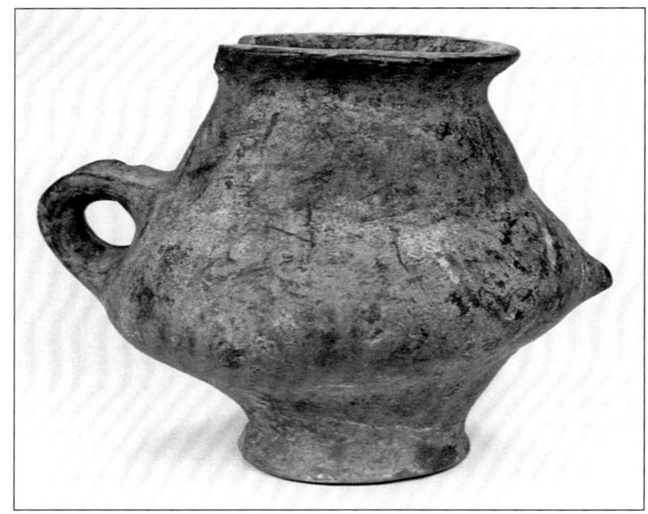

2
Etruscan Villanovan Single-handle Urn
8th century B.C.
H. 4 1/4 in. 10.8 cm; d. 5 7/8 14.9 cm; d. at lip 3 1/8 in. 8 cm
Gift of Frances W. English, 1979.1777

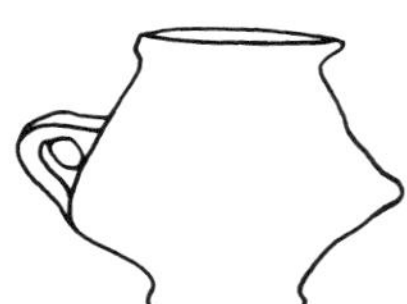

Condition: Intact. Much of surface shows heavy soil, debris obstructing much of original pigment. Chips and gouges at top rim, handle, and body. Lip has piece broken off and two chips.

Decoration: Gray brown clay with much wear. Slightly flaring lip gives way to slightly tapered neck. Poorly fashioned body augmented with three evenly spaced knobs that protrude from widest part of body. Single small grooved top handle.

Nineteenth-century archaeologists named this type of pottery after the town of Villanova near Bologna. Here archaeologists first recognized the urnfield culture of the Iron Age inhabitants of Etruria. The biconical and hut urns are used to bury the dead.

Unpublished. For shape and refined fabric, cf. CVA British Museum 7 (Great Britain 10), Etruria and Latium: Impasto and Bucchero, pl. 8, no. 5.

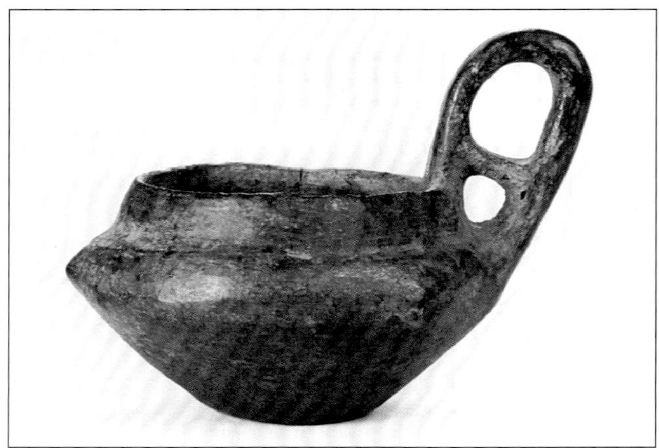

3
Etruscan Villanovan Urn with Double-loop Handle
8th–7th century B.C.
H. 2 15/16 in. 7.5 cm; w. 4 in. 10.2 cm; d. mouth 2 1/2 in. 6.3 cm; d. belly 3 1/2 in. 8.9 cm
Gift of Frances W. English, 1979.1143

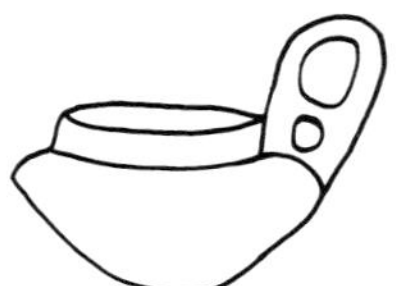

Condition: Intact. Highly abraded. Solidified debris covers majority of vessel. Tiny indentations dot surface.

Decoration: Undecorated and unpolished clay body of brownish red. Low vertical rim, biforal handle. Three protruding knobs symmetrically spaced around widest part of body, double-loop handles.

Unpublished. Cf. handle, size Copenhagen 5 (Danemark 5), pl. 193, no. 8; CVA British Museum 7 (Great Britain 10), Etruria and Latium, impasto and Bucchero, pl. 3, no. 10. Cf. three knobs in Fairbanks, Catalogue of Greek and Etruscan Vases,pl. 79, no. 598

4
Etruscan Villanovan Impasto Kyathos
8th–early 7th century B.C.
H. 5 1/4 in. 13.3 cm; D. 10 in. 25.4 cm
Gift of Jacqueline Ross, 1984.197

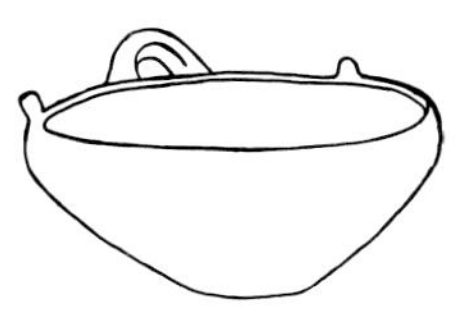

Condition: Intact, well preserved.

Decoration. Heavy clay fired black. Incised around the rim with hatched pendant triangles. Bowl features a single handle flanked by knobs. The kyathos is a type of lid used for covering an impasto biconical urn. DePuma suggests it may represent a female burial, since the helmet type cover suggests a male burial.

Unpublished. For similar kyathos with urn, see Richard DePuma, *Etruscan and Villanovan Pottery* (Iowa City, Iowa 1971), 8, cat. no. 5–6. The urn and kyathos are from the Dayton Art Institute, 68.61. For similar kyathos, cf. CVA Museo Pigorini Rome 1 (Italy 21), pl. 2, no. 9 and pl. 3, no. 14, although both examples lack flanking knobs.

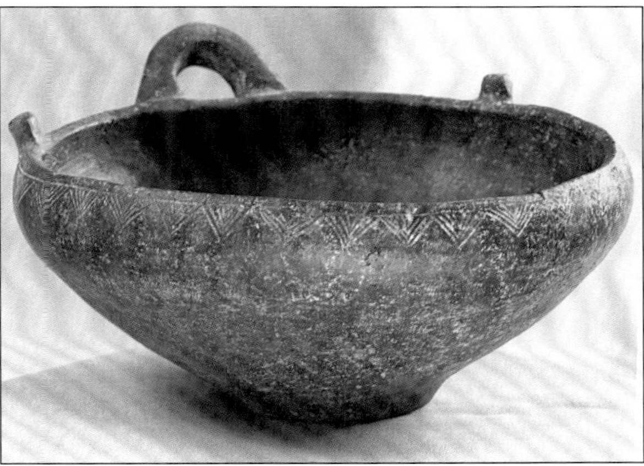

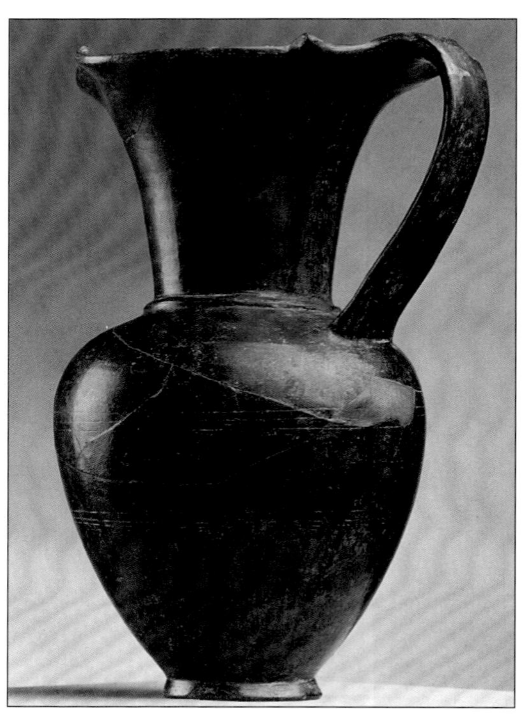

5
Etruscan Bucchero Olpe
Early period: 650–600 B.C.
H. 8 in. 20.3 cm; d. rim 4 1/2 in. 11.4 cm; d. with handle 5 5/8 in. 14.3 cm; d. without handle 4 1/2 in. 11.4 cm
Gift of Jacqueline Ross, 1984.195

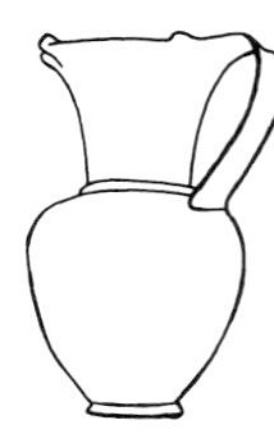

Condition: Broken and mended but complete.

Decoration: Clay has black polished surface. Ovoid body resting on low flat foot. Unusually tall neck with flaring lip and trefoil mouth; small spurs on rim on either side of ribbon handle. Bands of three and four incised lines around belly.

Bucchero is the characteristic type of Etruscan pottery. To produce the distinctive black color from red clay, the Etruscans fired the pot first in an oxidizing kiln, then closed off the supply of oxygen to form a reduction atmosphere. Vases were usually polished to produce the luster, and decoration limited to simple incising.

Unpublished. For general shape, cf. CVA British Museum 7 (Great Britain 10), Etruria and Latium: Impasto and Bucchero, pl. 21, no. 16 and CVA Copenhagen 5 (Danemark 5), pl. 212, no. 4.

6

Etruscan Bucchero Sottile Nikosthenic Amphora with Perforated Handles

650–575 B.C.

H. 8 3/8 in. 21.3 cm; d. rim 4 3/16 in. 10.6 cm; d. with handles 6 5/8 in. 16.8 cm; d. without handles 5 9/16 in. 14.2 cm

Gift of Jacqueline Ross, 1984.194

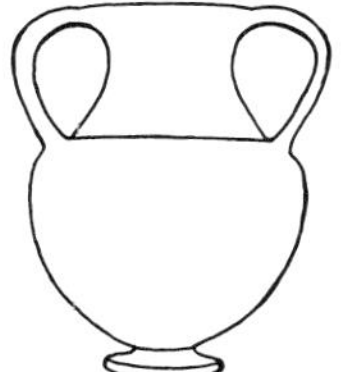

Condition: Intact, fine condition.

Decoration: Clay black-gray, surface polished and smooth. Ovoid body resting on flaring foot. Slightly flaring lip, perforated handles from lip to shoulder. The pierced handles show two felines in separate frames proceeding towards rim. Feline shape highlighted by removal of background. Central frieze zone created on body by two ridged horizontal lines. Within central zone, the three incised birds face right; one just left of center in front; another just right of handle on side A/B; and the third directly under handle on side B/A.

The Nikosthenic type is so called after the Athenian workshop of the potter Nikosthenes, who worked in the last third of the sixth century B.C. and specialized in the Etruscan market, using early Italian vase shapes rather than Greek.

Unpublished. Cf. DePuma, *Etruscan and Villanovan Pottery*,20, cat. no. 30. For handles, cf. CVA Tarquinia 2 (Italy 26), Bucchero, pl. 2, no. 4; CVA Villa Giulia, Rome 1 (Italy 1), pl.1, nos. 6,8. Cf. for similar shape E. von Mercklin "Etruskische Keramik im Hamburgishen Museum für Künst und Gewerbe," *Studi Etruschi* 9(1935): 318, pl. 46, no. 16. For similar incised birds we are grateful to Richard DePuma for calling our attention to Monika Verzár, "Eine Gruppe etruskischer Bandhenkelamphoren," *Antike Kunst* 16 (1973): 45–46 and to CVA Musée du Louvre 20 (France 31), pl. 29, no.1–3.

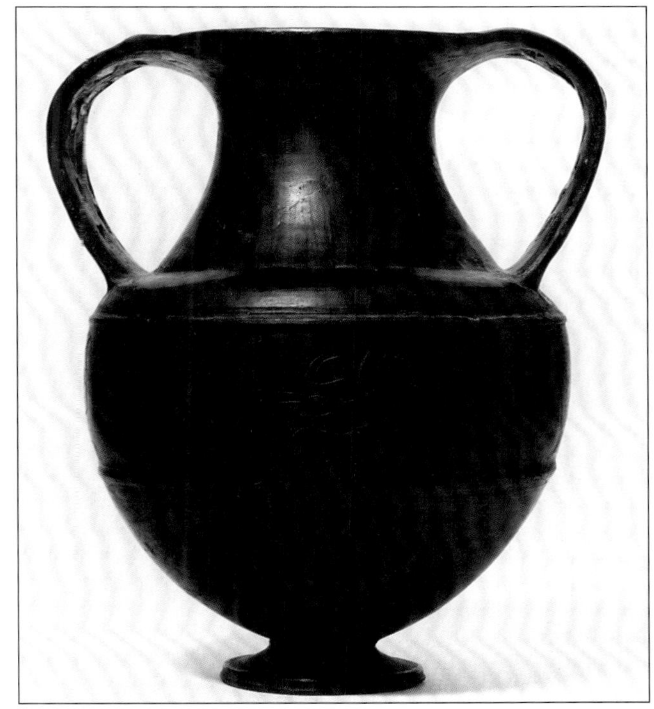

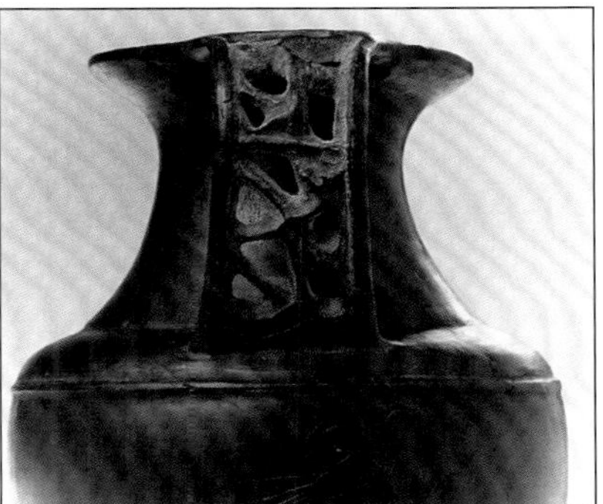

Detail of handle

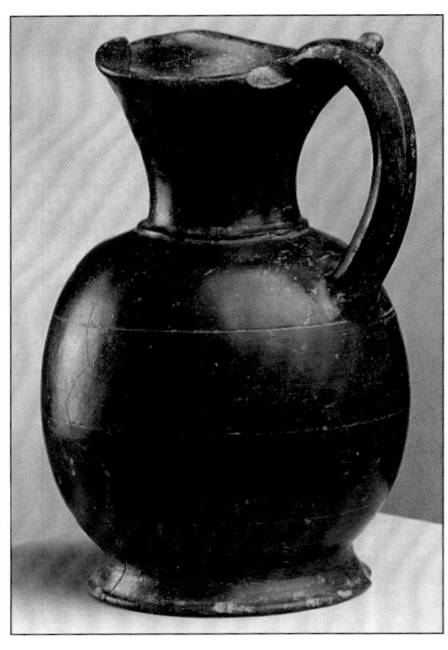

7
Etruscan Bucchero Olpe
Middle period 610–560 B.C.
H. 7 3/8 in. 18.7 cm; d. with handle 5 in. 12.7 cm; d. without handle 4 5/8 in. 11.7 cm; d. foot 3 11/16 in. 9.4 cm
Gift of Jacqueline Ross, 1984.196

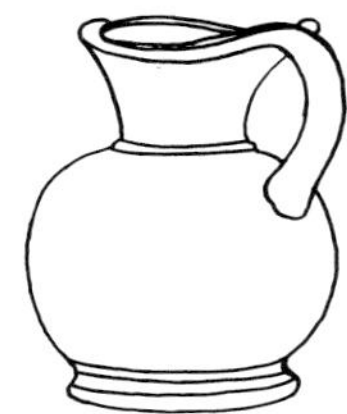

Condition: Broken, mended, surface pitting.

Decoration: Good black polish, trefoil mouth, round handle, two studs (one broken off) on rim on either side of handle. Three incised horizontal lines evenly spaced from just below handle to base, ridge where neck joins body.

Unpublished. For similar shape and features, cf. CVA British Museum 7 (Great Britain 10), group IV B a, pl. 22, nos. 4,5; CVA Copenhagen 5 (Danemark 5), pl. 212, no. 2.

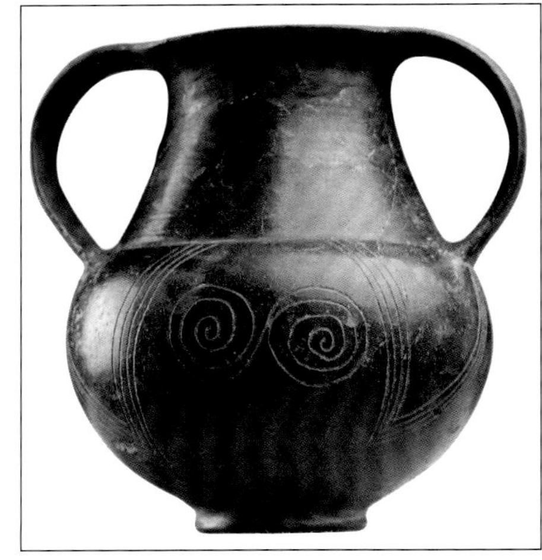

8
Etruscan Bucchero Sottile Miniature Amphora
Ca. 600 B.C.
H. 4 7/8 in. 9.8 cm; d. with handles 3 3/4 in. 9.5 cm; d. without handles 3 1/4 in. 8.3 cm; d. foot 1 1/4 in. 3.2 cm
Gift of Jacqueline Ross, 1984.198

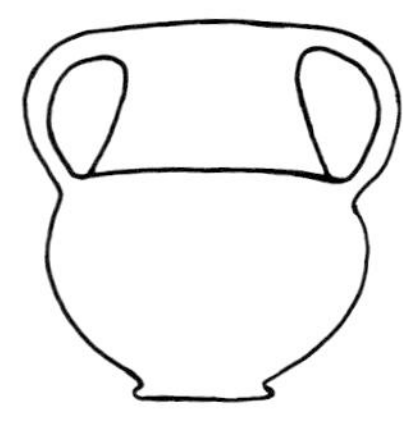

Condition: Mended handles and top of neck but intact, with minor surface pitting.

Decoration: Black gray clay with dull polish. Nikosthenic ribbon handles extend from slightly flaring rim to shoulder. Body decorated on both sides with incised reversed-spirals flanked by a group of parallel lines forming large V shapes.

Unpublished. For comparable decoration, DePuma, *Etruscan and Villanovan Pottery*, 14, cat. no. 18; CVA Copenhagen 5 (Danemark 5), pl. 196, nos. 3, 4, 5, 6; CVA British Museum 7 (Great Britain 10), Etruria and Latium: Impasto and Bucchero, pl. 5, no. 11, 14; pl. 13, no. 15, 17.

9
Etruscan Red Impasto Vase
Workshop in Caere
Ca. 2nd half of 7th century B.C.
H. 22 1/2 in. 57.2 cm; d. rim 6 11/16 in. 17.1 cm; d. foot 5 7/8 in. 14.9 cm; d. without handles 10 5/8 in. 26.8 cm; d. with handles 13 1/4 in. 33.7 cm
Harold F. Bishop Fund and Endowment Fund purchase, 1978.34, Bruce and Ingrid McAlpine, London

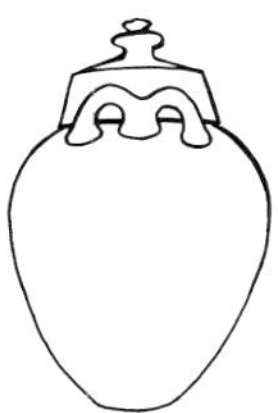

Condition: Exceptionally well-preserved vase.

Decoration: Horizontal bands of varying breadth are set off by tight parallel lines arranged in groups of four or five, with the exception of the lower portion of the lid and the base of the vase where the horizontal lines are comparatively thick, imparting a visual stability. Lower half of vase has two broad bands that carry equally spaced elongated solid triangles in contrasting creamy white paint and red impasto base; between handles at each side are two highly stylized birds that face right. A series of loose "s" motifs, inclined to the right, are set within a single narrow band on the lid and within two bands on the body, which frame the chief decorative zone for the upper half of the base. The continuous decorative band is composed of Orientalizing floral motifs: repeated pendant palmette and lotus motif that contrasts to the tendril-like curve that encloses the palmette, the diagonal petals, and the short horizontal and vertical dashes for both palmette and lotus.

This impasto jar is almost identical to one at the Musuem of Art and Archaeology, University of Missouri-Columbia (68.71); both these and six others excavated from a tomb in Caere are evidently from the same workshop.

Bibliography: Mario Del Chiaro, "An Early Etruscan Red Impasto Vase," Elvehjem *Bulletin* (1981–83): 29–31. Osmund Overby, ed. *Illustrated Museum Handbook: A Guide to the Collections in the Museum of Art and Archaeology, University of Missouri-Columbia* Columbia 1982), 32. Also see Robert L. Gordon, Jr., "Evidence for an Etruscan Workshop," *Muse* (Museum of Art and Archaeology, University of Missouri-Columbia) 5 (1971): 35–42.

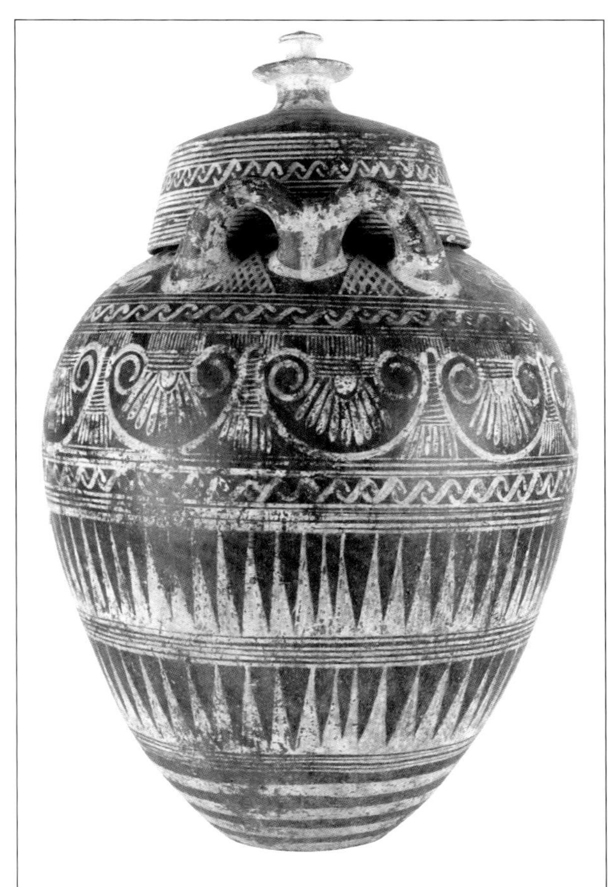

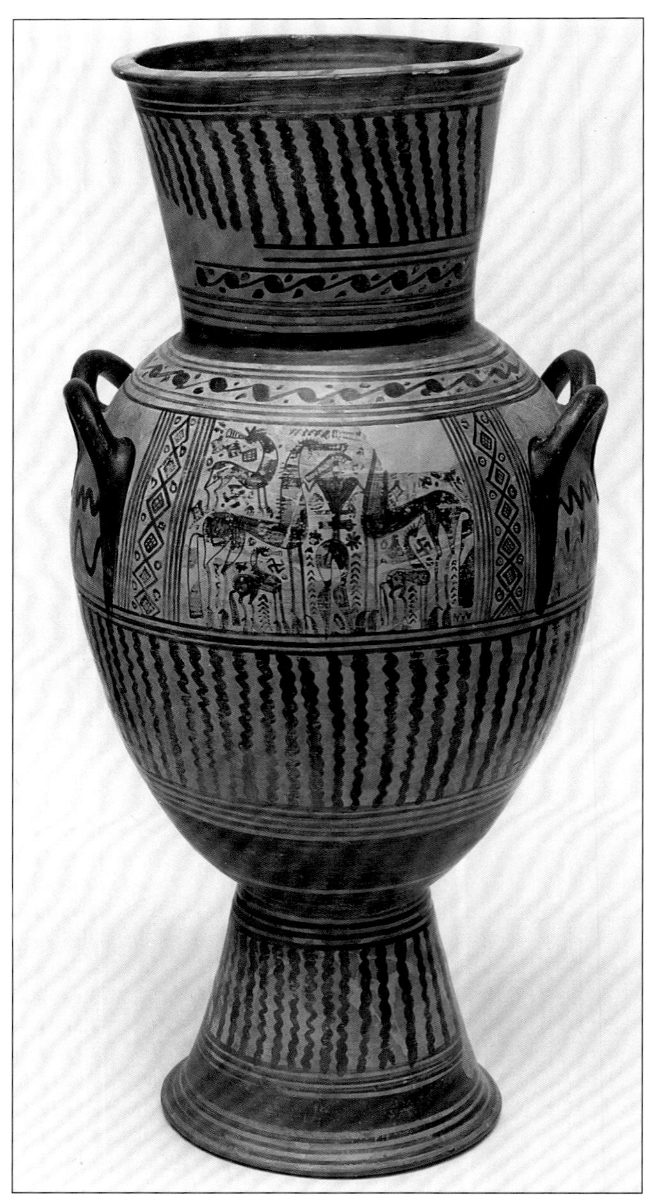

10

Boeotian Belly-handled Amphora (Group C)

Ca. 700–690 B.C.

H. 35 3/4 in. 91 cm; w. 16 1/2 in. 42 cm; d. rim 13 1/4 in. 33.8 cm; d. of base 10 13/16 in. 27.5 cm

Max W. Zabel Fund purchase, 68.19.1, Andre Emmerich Gallery, Inc. New York

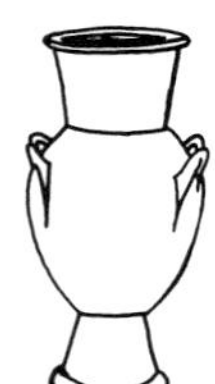

Condition: Amphora has been recomposed with some restoration in plaster.

Decoration: This pot is unusual because of monumental size and because motif of warrior between horses, derived from Attic models, does not occur on other Boeotian amphorae. On warm buff clay the decoration appears in reddish-brown glaze. There is a wide zone of thick, vertical, wavy lines on foot, lower body, and upper neck; above and below such zones are varying numbers of well-spaced, finely drawn lines in glaze. Broad areas in slip mark the join of the neck to body and body to foot. On panels the scene is the same on both sides: a warrior, wearing a helmet that is decorated with latticing, sword, and sheath at waist, stands between two horses facing him. Under each of these large horses is a small horse facing right. The one on the right in each scene appears to be nursing. Above the large horses are two goats, both with heads turned back. As typical in early Boeotian painting, horses have extended muzzles, thin legs, heavy hooves, and thick, tasseled tails. Filling ornament of swastikas, herringbone, small stars, lozenges, small dots, and circles.

Bibliography: H. Cahn, *Art of the Ancients* (New York 1968), 3, no. 1. Elvehjem *Bulletin* (1970–71): 42 (illus.). P. P. Kahane, "Ikonologische Untersuchungen zur griechischgeometrischen Kunst: der Cesnola-Krater aus Kourion im Metropolitan Museum," *Antike Kunst* 16.2 (1973): 137, pl. 29.4. A. Ruckert, *Fruhe Keramic Bootiens: form und Dekoraton der Vasen des spaten 8. und furhen 7 Jahrhunderts v. Chr. Antike Kunst* Beiheft 10 (Bern 1976), 90 pl. 13.4, no. BA 40, mentioned also on 19f., 55f. W. G. Moon and L. Berge, *Greek Vase-Painting in Midwestern Collections* (Chicago 1979), 4–5, cat. no. 4.

11
East Greek Trefoil Oinochoe
650–600 B.C.
H. 9 5/16 in. 23.6 cm; d. belly 8 in. 20.2 cm; d. foot 5 1/4 in. 13.4 cm
Evjue Foundation Fund purchase, 1979.79, Summa Galleries, Inc., Beverly Hills, Cal.

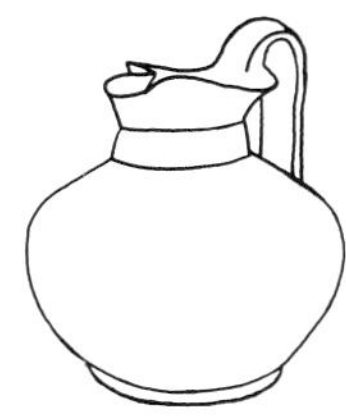

Condition: Intact. Some abrasion and large patches of brown and red pigment have worn away. White underpainting has worn away in small patches, especially at mouth, center of belly side A and at handle of vessel. Shallow, recessed chips in surface at neck. Brown solidified residue surrounds lip of mouth and base of foot.

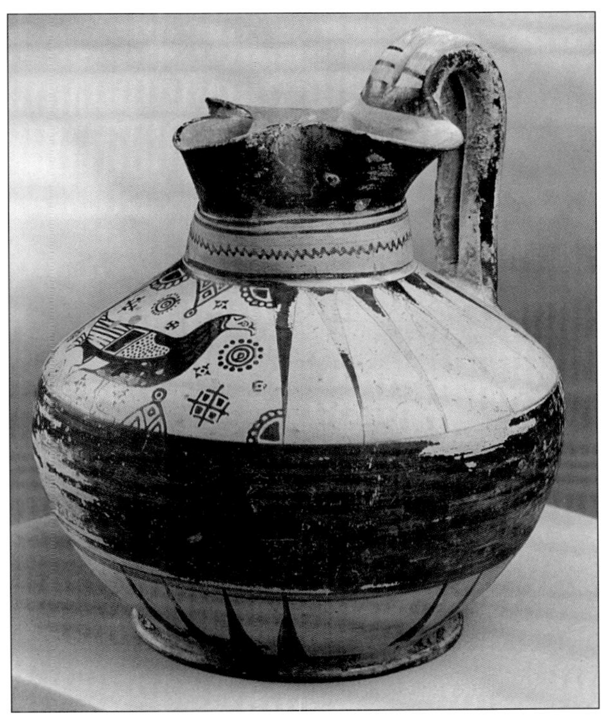

Decoration: The pot has flanged base and handle composed of two ribs. The black zigzag pattern on neck is banded on either side by lines of dark red glaze. On shoulder red and black rays alternate; central panel shows stylized bird (goose or partridge?) and various filling ornaments. Below red lines on black ground and black base rays arranged in groups of four. Red is added to bird neck and wing. The source of manufacture for such designs is thought to be either Samos or Rhodes.

Bibliography: The Summa Galleries, Inc., Catalogue no. 4: Ancient Vases (November 1978), pl.4. Cf. Moon, *Greek Vase-Painting in Midwestern Collections*, 16–17, cat. no. 11, for a similar shape and decoration on a vase from the Museum of Art and Archaeology, University of Missouri (71.11.3) that R. M. Cook dated to 600 B.C.

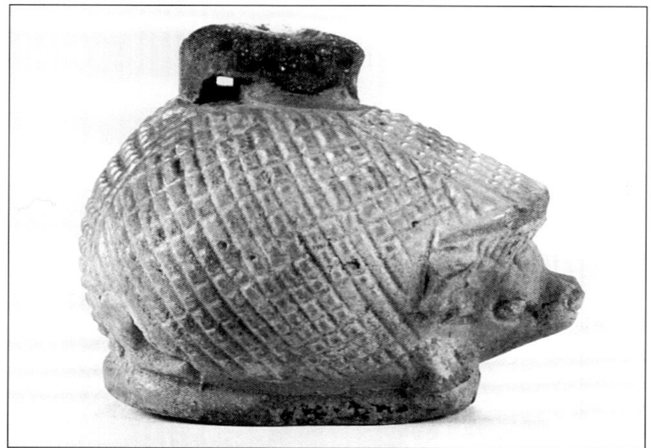

12
East Greek (Rhodes) Faience Hedgehog Vase
6th century B.C.
H. 1 7/8 in. 4.8 cm; l. 2 1/2 in. 6.4 cm
Gift of Bruce and Ingrid McAlpine, 1979.1119

Condition: Intact. Soil and abrasion throughout. Glaze badly worn at rim, lower sides, and base. Area just above hedgehog face heavily abraded. White and red pigment residue on underside.

Decoration: The hedgehog is shown squatting on an oval base with its front legs roughly indicated by narrow projections and its rear legs shown inorganically outside its coat. The nostrils and eyes are incised; the ears and nose are modeled. Incised lines sloping from back to front are crossed by similar pattern running from front to back, forming a gridlike pattern over the sides of the body. The coat is realistically shown as projecting above and forward over the head. The base is made of a hard whitish fabric, probably hand molded around sticks and covered with the blue, glasslike glaze.

Bibliography: Elvehjem *Bulletin* (1978–80): 82 (illus.). William Biers, "Ancient Figure Vases in the Elvehjem," Elvehjem *Bulletin* (1987–88):12–17.

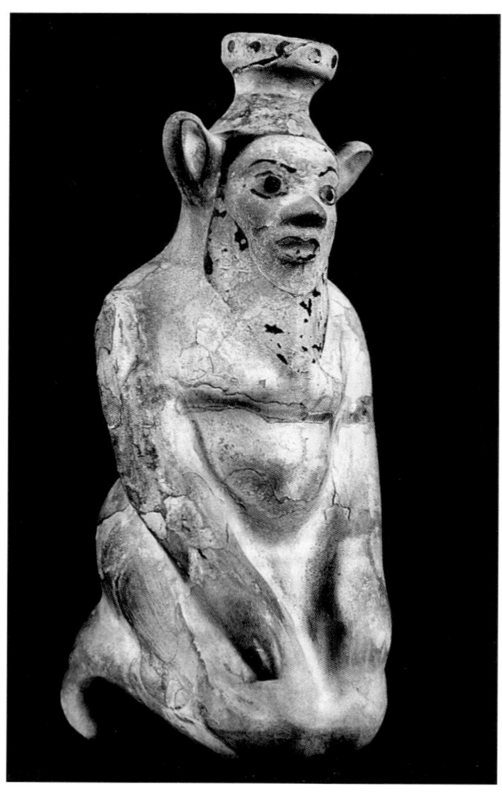

13
East Greek (Rhodes) Alabastron of Kneeling Satyr
6th century B.C.
H. 6 in. 15.2 cm
Elvehjem Museum of Art League Fund purchase, 1983.5

Condition: Intact but heavily restored. Paint has crackled and flaked throughout; at back of figure several layers of crackled paint visible. Whitish residue covers all. Repaired crack/ fracture at tip of head-dress.

Decoration: Soft modeled form with traces of black paint on eyes, eyebrows, and mouth. Also traces of black dots between lips and on beard. Top of head painted black, large oval ears edged with black paint, and aryballos mouth on head has black dots around edge and black tongues around filling hole. Biers notes, "this vase is important in that there is no other figure vase that can be considered its exact parallel."

Bibliography: William Biers, "Ancient Figure Vases in the Elvehjem," Elvehjem *Bulletin* (1987–88):12–17

14
East Greek Helmeted-head Aryballos
First half 6th century B.C.
H. 2 5/16 in. 5.9 cm; d. 2 1/4 in. 5.7 cm
Emily Mead Baldwin Fund purchase, 1979.121, Bruce and Ingrid McAlpine, London

Condition: Intact. Heavily abraded with loss or gouges at front tip rim, top right and bottom left edge, and right tip of helmet. Paint heavily crackled with some loss throughout.

Decoration: Warrior wearing black-glazed Ionian helmet with large, hinged cheek-piece, curved frontpiece over the forehead, flaring neck guard. Left side of vessel is misfired to red. Warrior's face is carefully formed with a prominent nose, narrow eyes, painted eyebrows, and mustache. Black paint is used for eyebrows, mustache, outline of eyes, and helmet; traces of red on top of the metopon, traces of white on hinges on right of helmet.

Plastic vases of this sort were used as scent or unguent bottles in the late seventh and early sixth centuries. They were probably made on Rhodes, where many have been found, or in Ephesos. Some have suggested that these small vases were funerary portraits of dead soldiers; others that they were souvenir gifts of military regiments.

Bibliography: William Biers, "Ancient Figure Vases in the Elvehjem," Elvehjem *Bulletin* (1987–88):12–17

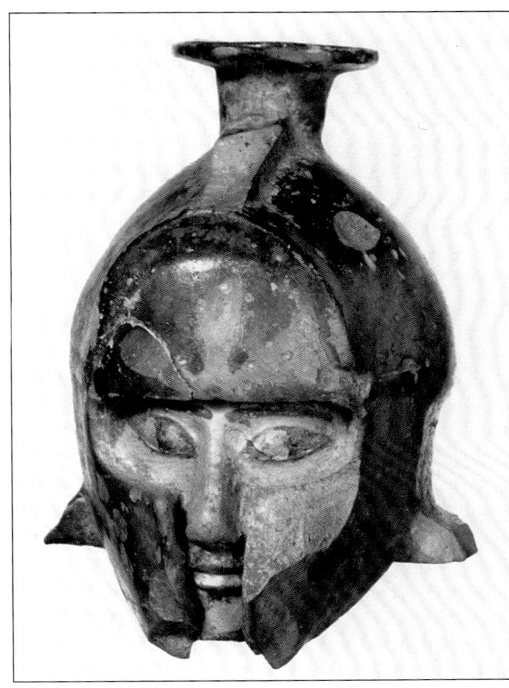

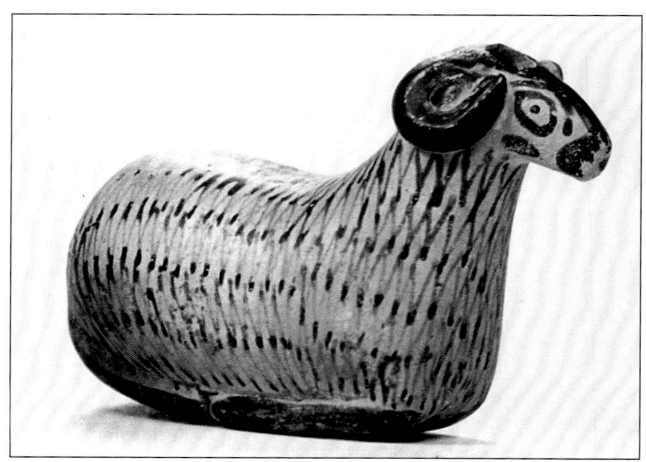

15
Corinthian Front-facing Ram Vase
Ca. 6th century B.C.
H. 2 1/8 in. 5.4 cm; l. 3 1/2 in. 8.9 cm
Humanistic Foundation Fund purchase, 1979.1117

Condition: Intact. Soil and abrasion throughout. Pigment largely intact but somewhat faded on side B. Abrasion and pigment loss at horns, face, and feet. Small shallow indentation just above back foot on side A.

Decoration: The body is made on the wheel; the head, feet, and tail are separately modeled and attached. The horns are rounded strips of clay applied behind the cylindrical head and curled around a central suspension hole. Horns and muzzle are covered by black glaze; the eye is portrayed by black dot in black oval with single curving line above. The pelt indicated by overall elongated lozanges.

Bibliography: William Biers, "Ancient Figure Vases in the Elvehjem," Elvehjem *Bulletin* (1987–88):12–17

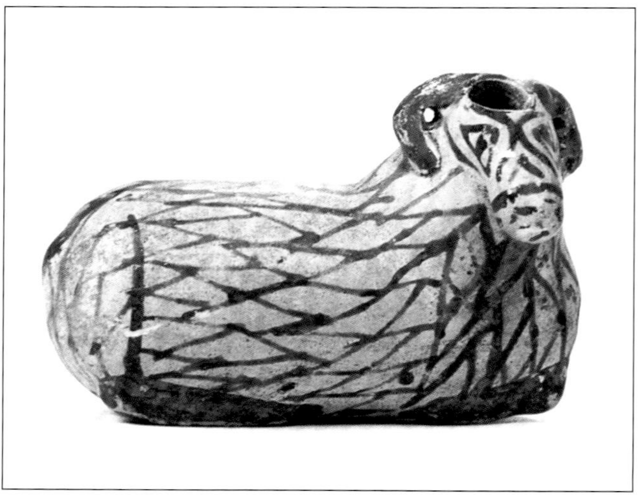

16
Corinthian Side-facing Ram Vase
6th century B.C.
H. 1 7/8 in. 4.8 cm; l. 2 7/8 in. 7.3 cm
Emily Mead Baldwin Fund purchase, 1979.1118

Condition: Intact. Soil and abrasion throughout. Fading and abrasion have caused loss of pigmentation at posterior end of figure. Side B shows pigment loss except for neck and feet, heavily abraded. Tip of face and horns show pigment loss.

Decoration: The body is made on the wheel; the head, feet, and tail are separately modeled and attached. The horns are rounded strips of clay applied behind the cylindrical head and curled around a central suspension hole. The horns and muzzle are covered by black glaze; the eye is portrayed by black dot in black oval with single curving line above. The pelt is indicated by overall elongated lozanges or netlike, zigzag lines.

Bibliography: William Biers, "Ancient Figure Vases in the Elvehjem," Elvehjem *Bulletin* (1987–88):12–17

17
Corinthian Olpe
Painter of Vatican 73 (Attribution by D. A. Amyx)
Early transitional, ca. 640–620 B.C.
H. 12 11/16 in. 32.2 cm; w. 6 3/8 in. 16.3 cm; d. of mouth 5 7/16 in. 13.8 cm; d. of base 3 9/16 in. 9.1 cm; d. foot 3 3/8 in. 8.2 cm
Gift of Mr. and Mrs. Arthur J. Frank, 1983.66, Summa Galleries, Inc. Beverly Hills, Cal.

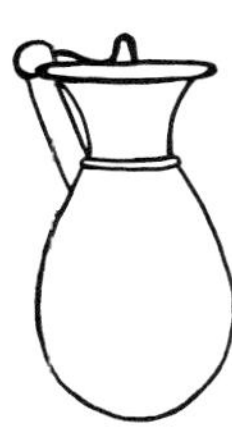

Condition: Mended breaks on neck; right rotelle broken and mended; glaze loss on rotelles, handles, neck, flaking of applied color. Slight restoration of the fabric in upper register and siren to right of center.

Decoration: Early transitional olpe has flaring lip, tripartite handle terminating in two rotelli at the lip, small ring foot. The neck is black-glazed with dot-rosettes in added red. Four bands of animal friezes all in black and red on buff-colored clay; the top focuses on swan with sphinx and panther facing; row two shows goat and panther flanked by a pair of licns with stag under handle; row three shows central swan between facing sphinxes, with panther, lion, goat, bull around; row four has goat under handles and lions, boars, stags. Black rosettes fill space between animals. The groundlines that that separate the friezes are black with an overlay of added red. There is zone of 20 rays at base; underneath the foot a central black dot within two concentric black circles.

The variety of animals and the arrangement of the swan between two sphinxes, as well as the careful attention to detail, are characteristic of the Painter of Vatican 73. This represents the transition phase between Protocorinthian animal style of the seventh century and the Corinthian vase painting that follows.

The attribution to the Painter of Vatican 73 has been disputed by C.W. Neeft, University of Amsterdam, in a letter to the museum.

Bibliography: Moon, *Greek Vase-Painting in Midwestern Collections*, 6–7, cat. no. 5. D. A. Amyx, *Corinthian Vase-Painting of the Archaic Period* (Berkeley and Los Angleles 1980), appendix II, no. A–26 bis.

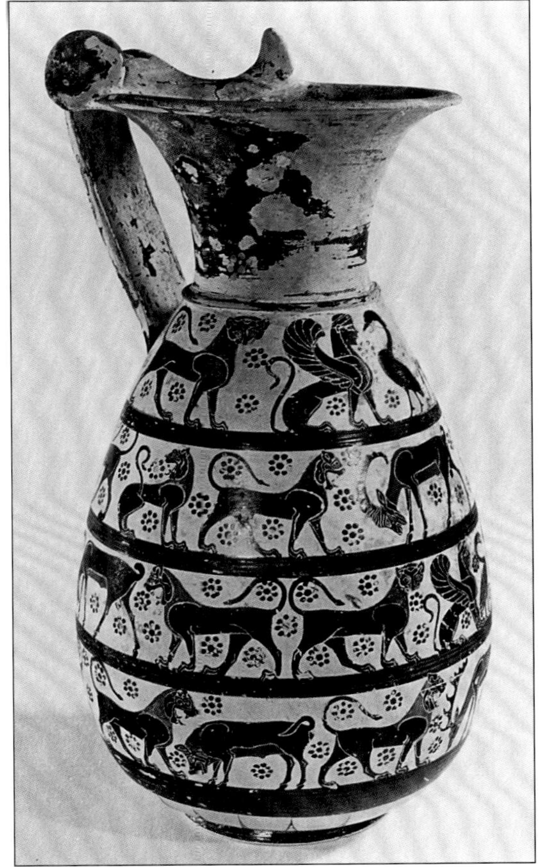

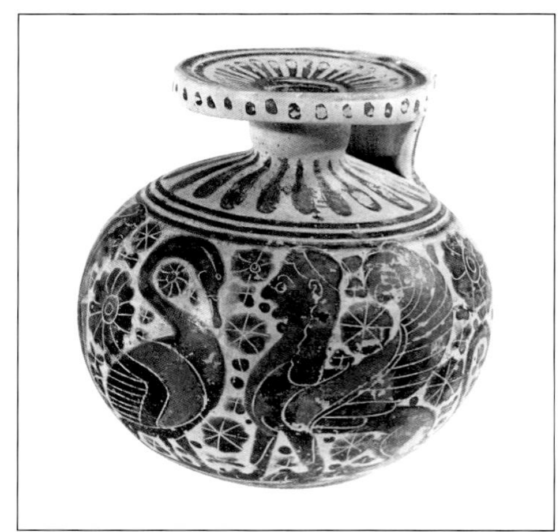

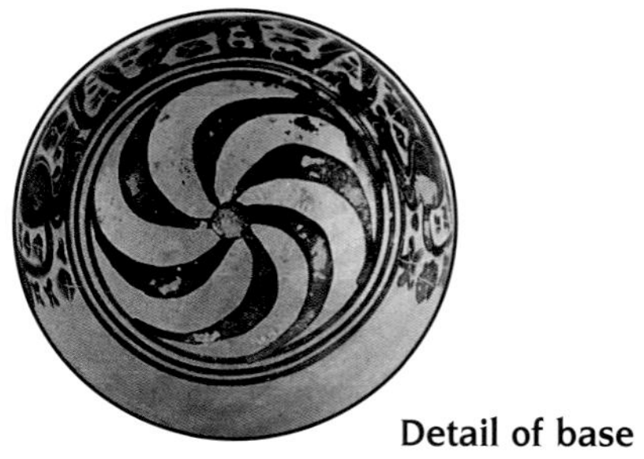

Detail of base

18
Protocorinthian Aryballos
Ca. 600 B.C.
H. 2 9/16 in. 6.5 cm; d. 2 9/16 in. 6.5 cm.
Ottilia Buerger Fund purchase, 1978.1, Bruce McAlpine, London

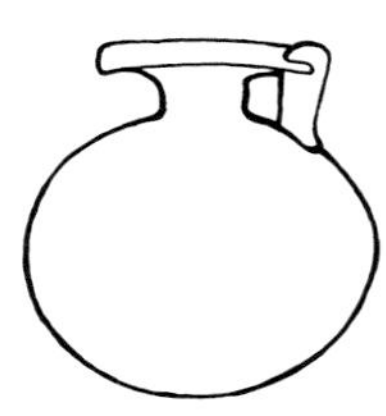

Condition: Intact. Surface abraded, areas of chipped and flaked glaze throughout. Red pigment faded. Thin whitish residue covers all.

Decoration: Round-bottomed globular aryballos with blaze dots on rim and tongue pattern on shoulder. Three concentric lines of slip frame the frieze of a central swan flanked by facing sphinxes and surrounded with floral and geometric fillers all in black and red pigment. The wings and facial features of swan and sphinxes are incised, as are many of the fillers. A pinwheel shape in black spirals from bottom center to concentric slip lines.

Unpublished.

19
Corinthian Broad-bottomed Oinochoe
Elvehjem Painter and the modern Shoe Lane Painter (Attribution by W. G. Moon, formerly attributed to the Lugano Painter by D. A. Amyx)
585 B.C.
H. 7 ¹/8 in. 18.3 cm; w. 6 ¹/2 in. 16.5 cm
Mary A. Grant Fund purchase, 70.3, auction, Munzen und Medaillen, Basel, Auktion 40, unknown private Basel or English collection

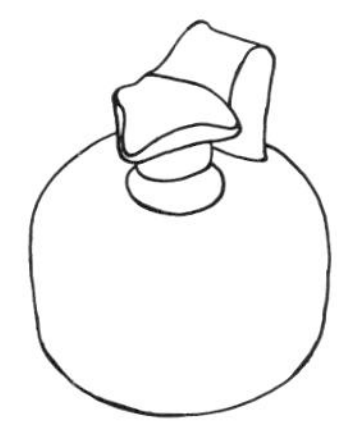

Condition: Intact, much of the glaze on neck and mouth has crackled and flaked. Areas are obviously repainted and lines of earlier incision are visible on bottom of the wing of the siren in the small animal frieze.

Decoration: Large animal frieze has central lion flanked by a pair of stags, panthers, and goats all facing the lion; a swan under the handle. A broad red band of glaze frames large frieze at top and bottom. Small frieze on shoulder has central swan with reverted head with pairs of facing sirens, goats, and swans; zone of 98 rays at base. All animals have added red and black.

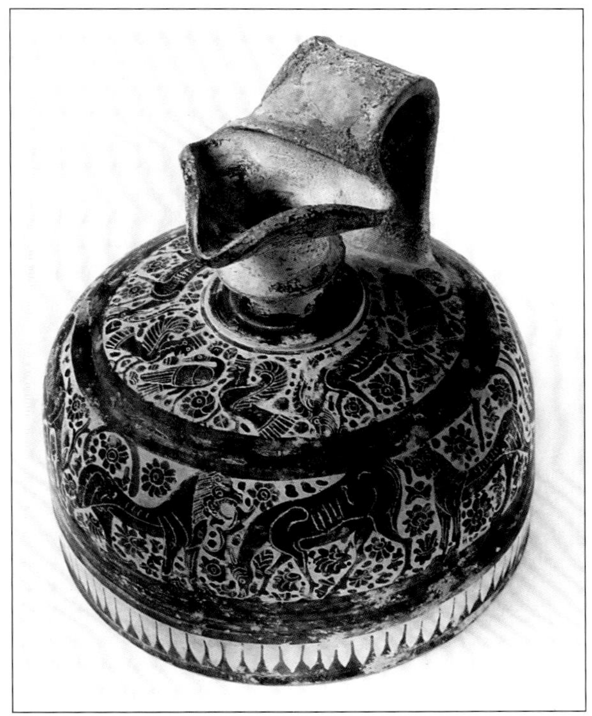

Bibliography: J. L. Benson, *Die Geschichte der Korinthischen Vasen* (Basel 1953), 47, pl. 9. H. Cahn, *Munzen und Medaillen AG Basel* Auktion 40 (13 December 1968), 21, lot 39, pl. 9. W. G. Moon, "A New Middle Corinthian Vase Painter in Madison: The Elvehjem Painter," *American Journal of Archaeology* 81 (1977): 382–89. Moon, *Greek Vase-Painting in Midwestern Collections*,28, cat. no. 17. Elvehjem *Bulletin* (1970–71): 42 (illus.).

For Shoe Lane Painter, see D. A. Amyx, "A Forged Corinthian Animal Frieze," *Bulletin of the Brooklyn Museum* 21.2 (1960), 9–13. Amyx, *Corinthian Vase-Painting of the Archaic Period*, 221.

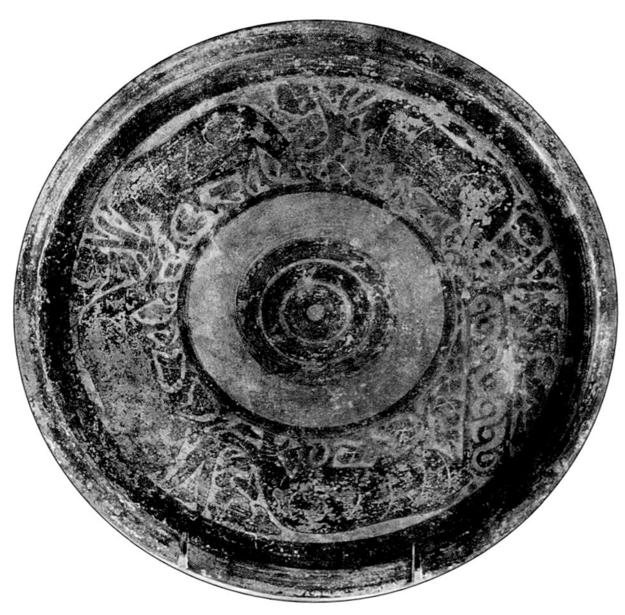

20
Etrusco-Corinthian Footed Dish
Poughkeepsie Group of the Workshop of "Senza graffito" Painter (Tarquinia) (Attribution by J. G. Szilágyi)
Ca. 580–560 B.C.
H. 1 7/8 in. 4.8 cm; d. 10 3/8 in. 26.3 cm; d. foot 3 5/8 in. 9 cm
Transfer from Department of Classics, 1978.250

Condition: Intact, but 1 1/2 inch gash in right side. Highly abraded and soiled; much of red chipped or dulled by grime. White residue at underside of belly and along left side of rim.

Decoration: Tondo shows three concentric dark slip circles, a reserved circle banded by a frieze of four poorly drawn stags facing right with lowered heads and antlers almost lost in the filler of stylized vegetation. A simple guilloche pattern is inserted awkwardly between two of the animals.

Unpublished.

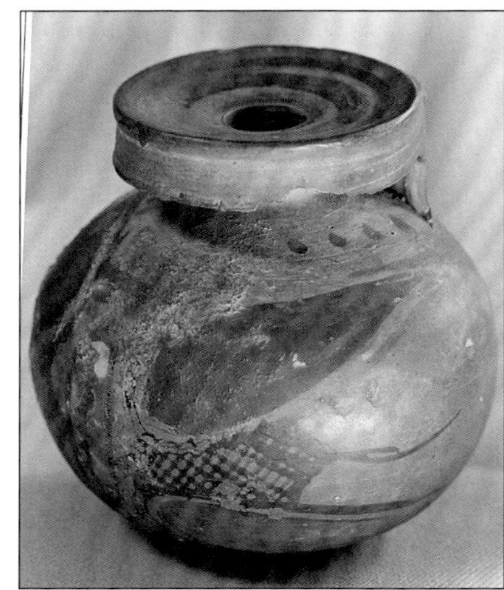

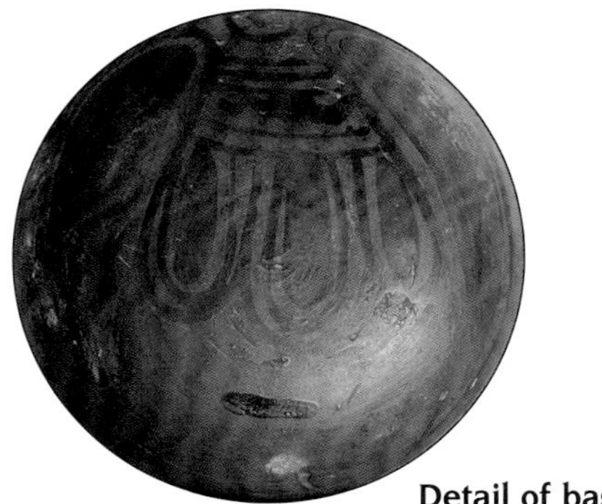

Detail of base

21
Corinthian Aryballos
Ca. 575–550
H. 3 1/4 in. 8.3 cm
Bequest of Eloise Gerry, 1971.48

Condition: Slight chip on rim, abrasion of the mouth, much of surface darkened by burning or chemical reaction.

Decoration: Round-bottomed globular aryballos. Black concentric circles around mouth. Outline quatrefoil motif consists of four stylized and elongated leaf shapes that radiate diagonally from a vertical ovoid shape at the front center of the vase and extend to back. At the center of the oval is an undulating line; above the oval, connecting the upper two foils, is a thick band from which arise several short spikes. Touching the sides of the oval and linking the foil-pairs are patches of outlined cross-hatching. At back of vase is start of dilute orangish glaze, made from three crossing brush strokes. A row of dark dots on shoulder.

Unpublished

22
Attic Black-figure Kylix with Dancing Komasts
KY Painter (Attribution by W. G. Moon)
Ca. 580–570 B.C.
H. 3 15/16 in. 10.5 cm; d. at mouth 7 15/16 in. 19.8 cm; d. with handles 10 5/8 in. 27 cm; d. foot 3 1/8 in. 8 cm
Anonymous Fund and Humanistic Foundation Fund purchase, 1979.310, Kurt Deppert, Frankfurt, Germany

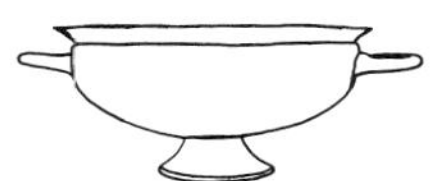

Condition: Reassembled with some restoration in plaster on each side of vase and on off-set lip.

Decoration: Sides A and B show three padded dancers facing the center away from the handles, with heads lowered. The central figure also has arms lowered but flanking figures have one arm raised and one lowered. There are rosettes on the off-set lip, and under each handle an arrangement of a palmette fan atop lotus flower. Red is added to torso and buttock pads of dancers, alternate petals of rosettes and palmette fans and fans within lotus flowers, cuffs of lotus flowers, hearts and roots of palmettes. The clay is warm orange; the black glaze thick and rich. Interior is black glazed.

Bibliography: Moon, *Greek Vase-Painting in Midwestern Collections*, 39, cat. no. 24.

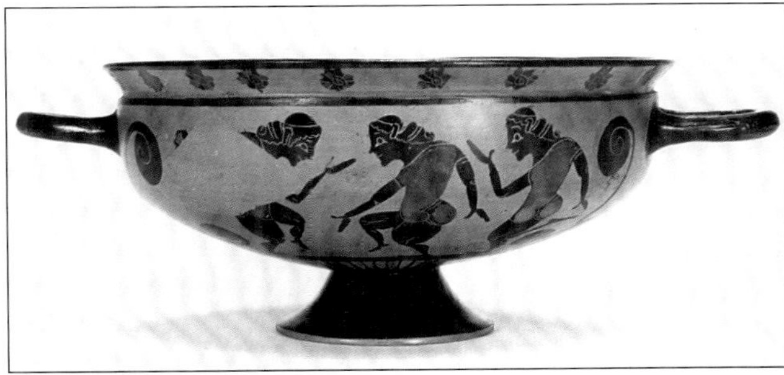

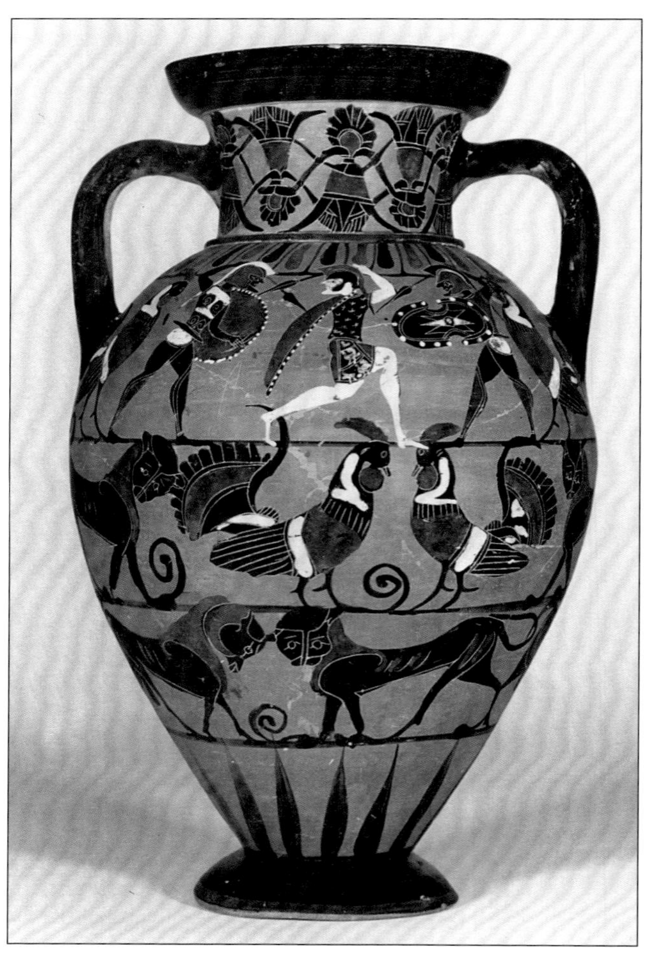

23
Attic [Tyrrhenian group] Black-figure Neck Amphora
Goltyr Painter
Ca. 565–550 B.C.
H. 15 1/2 in. 39.5 cm; d. at lip 6 1/8 in. 15.5 cm; d. at foot rim 4 11/16 in. 11.9 cm; d. with handles 9 1/4 in. 23.5cm
Gift of Mr. and Mrs. Arthur J. Frank, 1985.99, Summa Galleries, Beverly Hills, Cal.

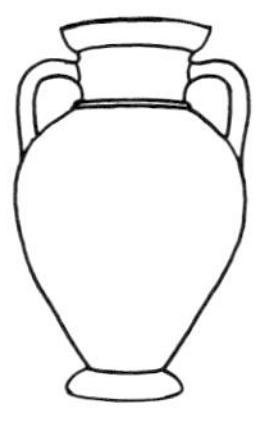

Condition: Reassembled from fragments. Repainted along seams of fragments. Glaze chipped and scratched in many areas. Abrasion and pigment loss at handles and mouth. Side B of lip has lost black glaze.

Decoration: Ovoid neck amphora with echinus lip and foot and round handles; decorated in black-figure with much added red and white. Lotus-and-palmette festoon encircles the neck. On the shoulder, tongue pattern alternating red and black. The body is decorated with three figured bands on each side. Side A, from the top: Amazonomachy flanked by roosters; two roosters facing, between panthers; panther and ram, facing. Side B, from the top: Komast between swans between sphinxes; panther between rams; panther followed by male figure (Hermes?) between ram and panther. Below, sixteen base rays.

Bibliography: Summa Galleries, Inc., Catalogue No. 5: Ancient Art, cat. no. 2. Cf. J. D. Beazley, *Attic Black-Figure Vase-Painters* (Oxford 1956), 94 ff.; J D. Beazley, *Paralipomena: Additions to Attic Black-Figure Vase-Painters and to Attic Red-Figure Vase Painters* (Oxford 1971),196 f; H. Thiersch, *"Tyrrhenische" Amphoren* (Leipzig 1899); D. von Bothmer, "The Painters of 'Tyrrhenian' Vases," AJA 48 (1944): 161–170.

24
Attic Black-figure Siana Cup
The Red/Black Painter (Attribution by J. T. Haldenstein)
Ca. 555 B.C.
H. 4 1/8 in. 10.5 cm; d. with handles 11 1/4 in. 29.2 cm; d. without handles 8 1/2 in. 21.9 cm; d. foot 3 1/8 in. 7.9 cm
The Ottilia Buerger Fund and Lynn Ashley Fund (Art Collections Fund) purchase, 1983.7, Mrs. Muriel Clifton, Beloit, Wis., 1964; Galerie Heidi Vollmoeller, Zurich

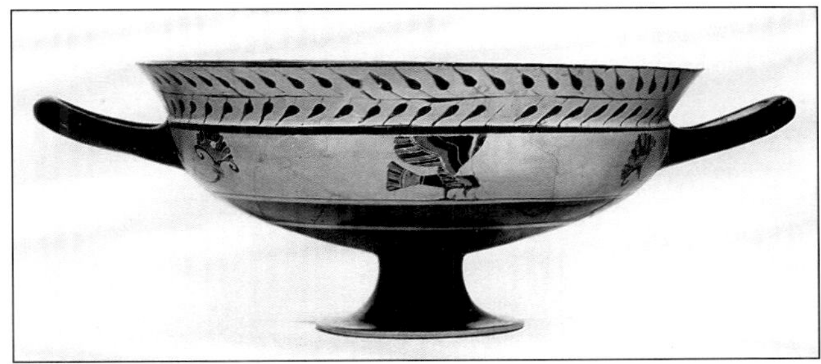

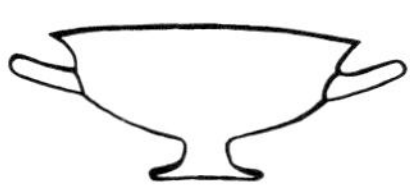

Condition: Reassembled from fragments; no missing pieces but several fragments repainted. Exterior side A included repainted fragment that interrupts rooster and myrtle wreath. Interior also shows repainted patches around palmettes encircling rooster.

Decoration: Deep, slightly bulging bowl has angular, offset lip. The handles rise almost to the height of the bowl; the foot is low and has sharply spreading profile that flows into the foot-plate. The Siana cup is named for the site in Rhodes where it was first noted. On both sides a displaying siren faces right, tail feathers and wing feathers outlined by incised lines and broad band of red added to wing; myrtle wreath in black decorates lip. On the interior, covered by black glaze except for tondo where rooster faces right, surrounded by three glaze lines and upright lotus bud chain and three additional glaze lines. Red is added to body, tail and alternate tail feathers, crest and comb; red also added to lotus buds.

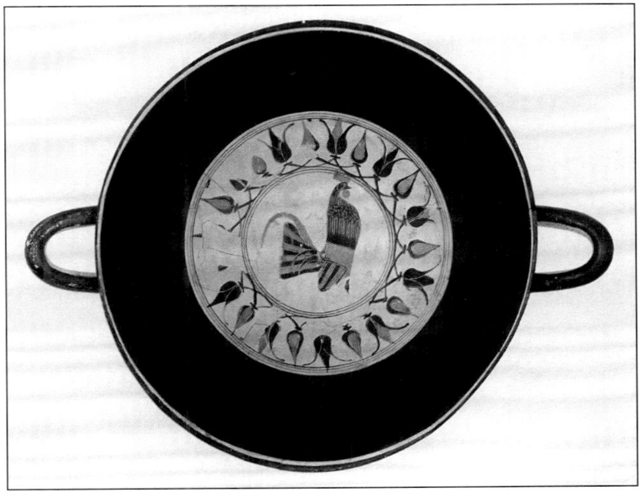

Interior

Bibliography: J. T. Haldenstein, "Four Attic Black-figure Cups at the Elvehjem," Elvehjem *Bulletin* (1989–91): 6–12.

25
Attic Black-figure Little Master Band Cup
Painter of the Boston Polyphemos (Attribution by J. T. Haldenstein)
Ca. 550 B.C.
H. 5 5/8 in. 14.3 cm; d. with handles 10 13/16 in. 27.9 cm; d. without handles: 8 7/16 in. 21.4 cm; d. foot 3 7/8 in 9.9 cm
Gift of Mr. and Mrs. Arthur J. Frank, 1981.134, Munzen und Medaillen, AG, Basel, Switzerland

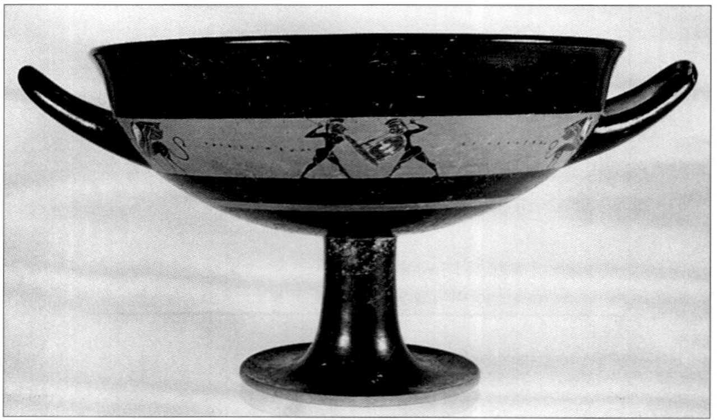

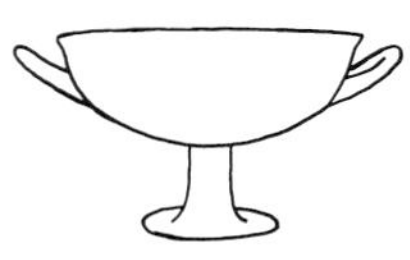

Condition: Intact. Reattached handle shows large crack. Foot reattached and repaired in antiquity. Painted surface highly abraded; extensive scratching and crackling throughout. Hardened white debris featured prominently in interior. Projecting chunk of plaster at base of interior surrounded by crack sealed with transparent hardened substance.

Description: Thin-walled, deep-bowled band cup with trumpet-shaped foot that is higher than a Siana cup. The bowl rises to the rim in continuous curve. Sides A and B each have a pair of dueling warriors, one with a Boeotian shield, the other a round shield, flanked by tiny Xaire inscriptions that salute the drinker but degenerate into nonsense. Shields, helmets, and breasts are highlighted with red; white is picked out for shield ornament and helmet crests. Incision outlines shields, helmet crests, spears, and various body parts, and wings of sphinxes. Sphinxes at handles turn heads back towards warriors. Interior tondo is reserved medallion. The battling hoplites are watched by handle sphinxes who raise paws in a triumphant gesture.

Bibliography: Munzen und Medaillen, *Kunstwerke der Antike* (March 14–15, 1975),47, cat. no. 124, illus p. 22. J. T. Haldenstein, "Four Attic Black-figure Cups at the Elvehjem," Elvehjem *Bulletin* (1989–91): 6–12. For Painter of the Boston Polyphemos, see ABV, 198–99.

26
Attic Black-figure Siana Cup
Griffin-Bird Painter
545 B.C.
H. 4 3/8 in. 11.2 cm; d. with handles 10 in. 25.4 cm;
d. without handles 7 1/2 in. 19 cm; d. foot 2 3/4 in. 7 cm
Gift of Mr. and Mrs. Arthur J. Frank, 1985.96, Jacques Schulman, B.V., Amsterdam

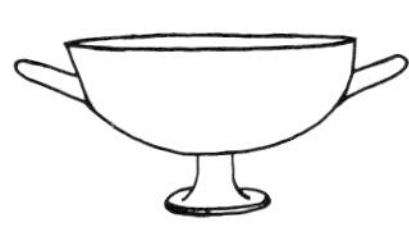

Condition: Reassembled. Prominent seam runs diameter of belly below animal motif. Paint cracked and flaked around foot of base and at handles. Swans and griffin-birds also show some paint loss. Exterior side B shows uneven pigmentation with bleached spot on lower belly. Some repainting on belly and tondo.

Decoration: The bowl is deep with offset lip and short, stubby handles. The foot is tighter than the usual Siana cup foot, and the rest plate broader, giving the cup a sturdy appearance and accounting for a late date in the painter's cup sequence. Side A shows three sirens and one griffin-bird facing left; side B has two sirens and two griffin-birds; white is added to wing, faces, and necks of sirens and breast and wings of griffin-birds. Red is added to tails and wings. In interior, in a reserved medallion encircled by a ring of black-and-red glaze, a frontal-faced panther stands at attention, body facing right. Incised lines mark face, legs, and rump of panther.

John Boardman describes Griffin-bird Painter as "...mainly satisfied with rather careless animals and florals, and his tondos lack fancy borders. But he was prolific, and the monster from which he takes his name was also the hallmark of a large group of cheap contemporary Corinthian cups." (ABFV, 33)

Bibliography: *Verkoplijst Met Vaste Prijzen* (Fixed-Price list), List 214, October 1978, Jacques Schulman B.V., Keizersgracht 448, Amsterdam. J. T. Haldenstein, "Four Attic Black-figure Cups at the Elvehjem," Elvehjem *Bulletin* (1989–91): 6–12. for Griffen-Bird Painter, see ABV, 71–74.

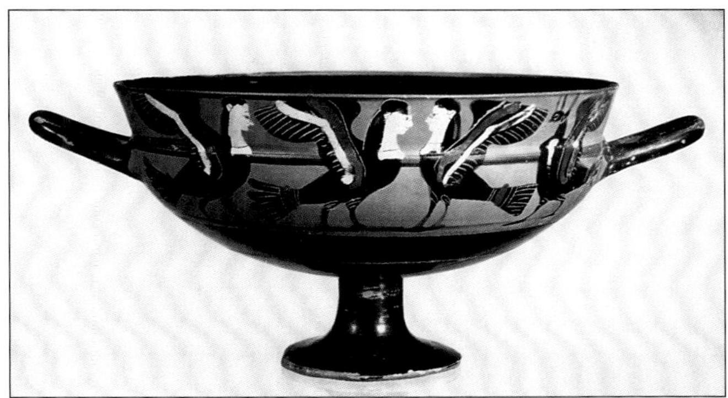

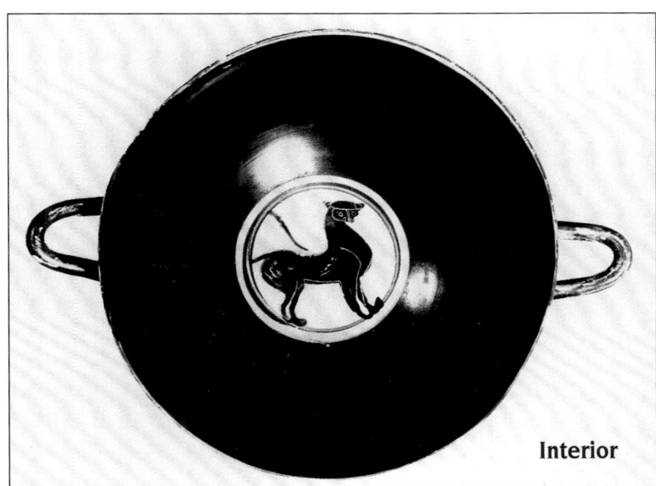

Interior

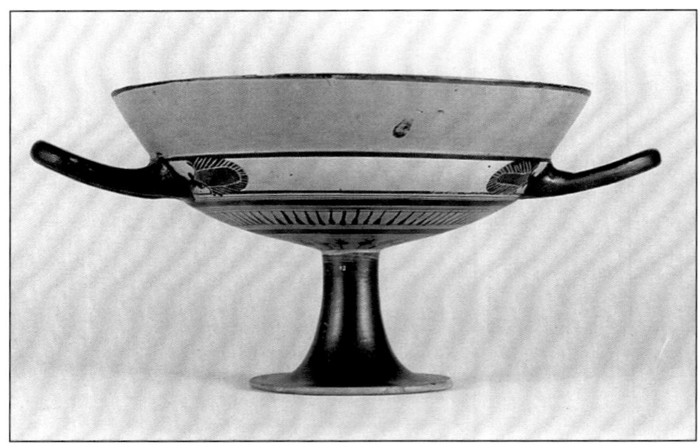

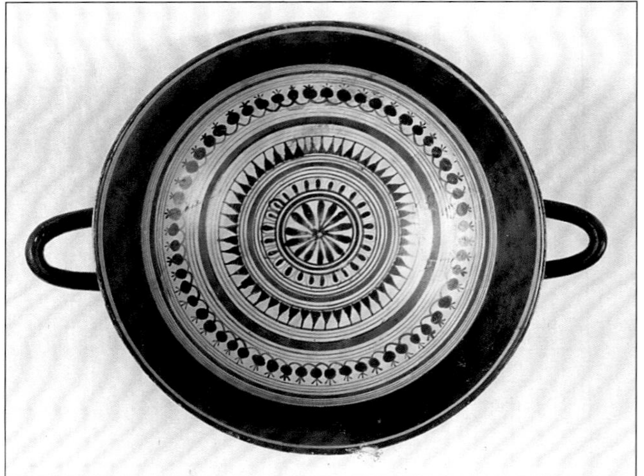

Interior

27
Attic Kylix in the "Decorated" Style
The Rider Painter (active ca. 570–535 B.C. in Laconia)
Ca. 540 B.C.
H. 4 5/8 in. 11.8 cm; d. with handles 9 11/16 in. 24.8 cm; d. at rim 7 3/16 in. 18.2 cm; d. foot 3 1/8 in. 7.8 cm
Fairchild Foundation Fund and Endowment Fund purchase, 1975.6, Munzen und Medaillen, A.G. Basel

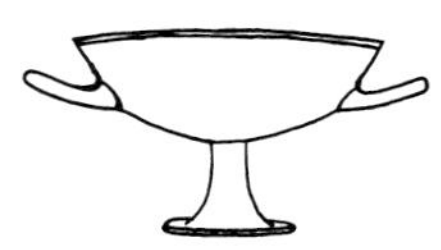

Condition: Reassembled. Repainted along seams of fragments. Exterior side A shows rust-colored patch of soil from lip to belly; side B shows teardrop-shaped patch of rust stain at top of belly.

Decoration: Interior, floral at center in three concentric lines of glaze, a band of egg-and-dot pattern, six glaze lines, a band of rays, seven lines of red glaze of varying widths, a lotus chain. Exterior shows fan palmettes at handles, beneath several lines of varying widths a band of rays, additional lines, and at base of what may be lotus buds.

Bibliography: Munzen und Medaillen, Auktion 51, *Kunstwerke der Antike* (14–15 March 1975) lot no. 113. Elvehjem *Bulletin* (1974–75): n.p. (illus.).

28
Attic Black-figure Neck Amphora
Euphiletos Painter (Attribution by J. D. Beazley)
Ca. 530 B.C.
H. 12 3/8 in. 31.5 cm; d. with handle 8 1/4 in. 21 cm; d. without handle 7 7/8 in. 17.7 cm; d. foot 3 15/16 in. 10 cm
Gift of Mr. and Mrs Arthur J. Frank, 68.14.2, Hesperia Art, Philadelphia, Penn.

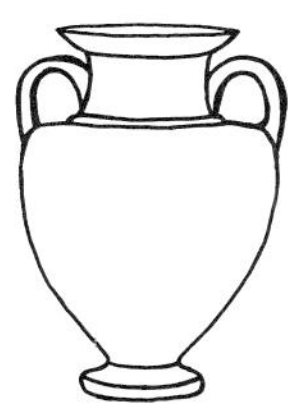

Condition: Intact. Cracking and flaking of paint throughout, especially at top rim, handles, and top of foot. Red and white paint appear soiled and abraded on side A and white on side B.

Decoration: Under handles four palmettes are connected by tendrils with three-point lotus bud in center. At the base of the neck is a narrow band of alternating black and dark red tongue pattern. The neck has a circuit of large lotus buds. Side A shows Herakles battling the Nemean lion, attended by Athena on the right and probably Herakles' nephew Iolaos on the left, gripping one black and one white club. Athena's large shield, which covers most of her body, is rimmed in dark red with a fig-leaf emblem in white. She is taller than the mortals, and her high-crested Athenian helmet breaks through the tongue pattern at the base of the vase's neck. Her skin areas have applied white, a convention denoting a female. She carries a spear and wears a peplos with a shorter overgarment that was once dark red. Side B has a central warrior with a high-crested Corinthian helmet and shield with a chariot's car in white. Two frontal horses with youthful barefoot riders facing away from center flank the central warrior. The two soldiers wear white chitons or tunics and have short hair bound with a fillet; one grasps single reins in front of the horse's head, the other double reins from behind.

The Euphiletos Painter takes his name from a love inscription (*Euphiletos kalos*) that appears on the shield of Athena on a Panathenaic prize amphora, London B134.

Bibliography: *Hesperia Art Bulletin* 22.2 (n.d.): 3, illus. 2. W. G. Moon, "A Black-figure Neck-amphora by the Euphiletos Painter," Elvehjem *Bulletin* (1971–72): 8–15. For vases by the Euphiletos Painter also showing Herakles and the Nemean lion, CVA Bibliothèque Nationale, Paris 2 (France 10), pl. 58, nos. 3, 4, 8 and CVA Villa Giulia, Rome 1 (Italy 1), pl. 6, nos. 1–3.

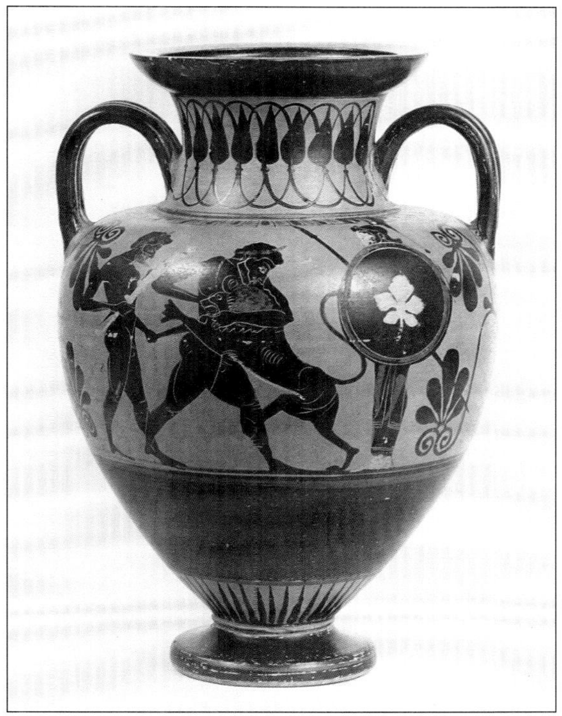

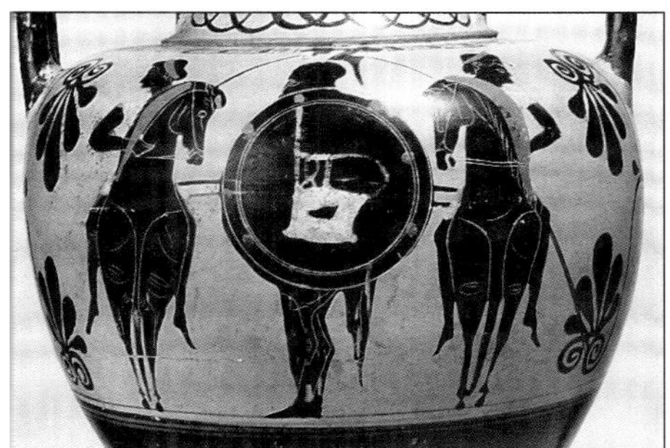

Detail of side B

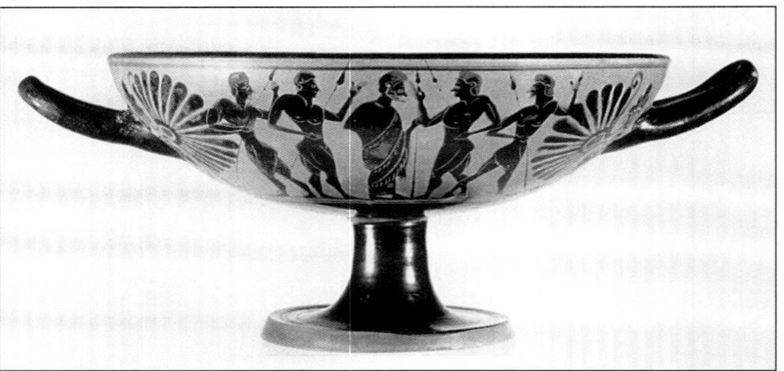

29
Attic Black-figure Kylix (Type A cup: FP class)
The Painter of the Nicosia Olpe, now conflated with the Painter of Louvre F28 (Attribution by J. T. Haldenstein)
Ca. 520 B.C.
H. 4 9/16 in. 11.6 cm; d. with handles 12 3/16 in. 31 cm; d. without handles 9 3/16 in. 23.3 cm; d. foot 4 3/8 in. 10.6 cm
Gift of Mr. and Mrs. Arthur J. Frank, 1981.133, Robert J. Myers, New York, N.Y.

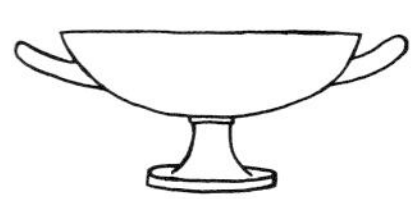

Condition: Largely intact but five-inch patch above handle and eight-inch section along belly have been reassembled. Repainted along fragment seams. Handles abraded. Side B shows abrasion and pigment loss on belly.

Description: The shallow bowl has a plain, not offset, lip with handles that rise to the height of the rim. The low foot with fillet at the top acts as cushion between bowl and foot. A large horizontal palmette at the handles springs from two smaller palmettes. Sides A and B each have five figures, four nude, beardless youths with spears and one upraised arm and a central bearded male leaning on a spear. The two parties of spear-throwers seem to be appealing to the central figure for a decision, perhaps in the spear-throwing contest. These may be four athletes with their older, bearded trainer. The youths wear purple red medallions on side B but not on side A. Red slip is added to hair, beards, chests, and the central figure's tunic. Incised lines mark eyes, ears, hair, limbs, chests, collarbones, and the fringe on the tunic on side B.

Bibliography: Myers/Adams Auction 8 (1974), cat. no. 103. J. T. Haldenstein, "Four Attic Black-figure Cups in the Elvehjem," Elvehjem *Bulletin* (1989–91): 6–12. For Painter of Louvre F28, see ABV 199; for Painter of Nicosia Olpe, see ABV 452, 53.

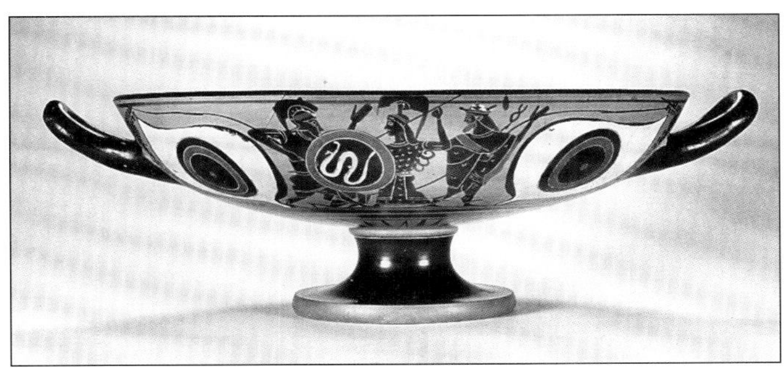

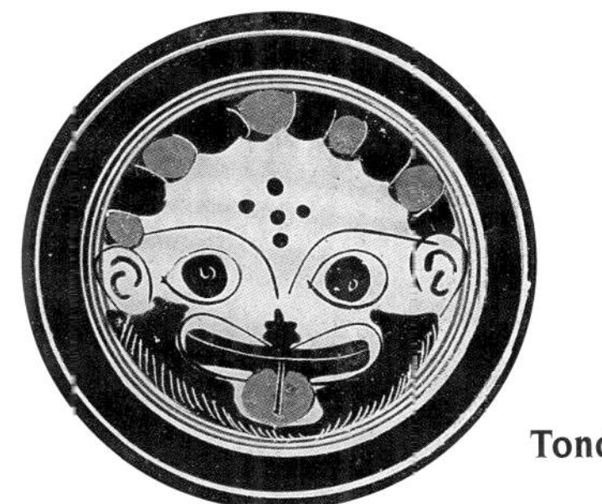

Tondo

30
Attic Black-figure Eye-Cup
Ca. 520 B.C.
H. 4 3/8 in. 11.2 cm; d. with handles 14 in. 35.5 cm; d. without handles 11 1/4 in. 28.4 cm; d. foot 4 3/8 in. 11.3 cm
Gift of Mr. and Mrs. Arthur J. Frank, 1985.97, Summa Galleries, Beverly Hills, Cal., Private collection, Switzerland

Condition: Mended from a few large fragments, some abrasion of glaze on handles.

Decoration: The broad and shallow bowl sits on a stocky stem; the base has a rather thick foot-plate that flows into the stem in an abrupt curve. The decoration on sides A and B are nearly identical.

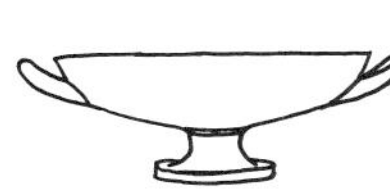

Figures stand between the eyes that have pointed tear gland and pointed upper, outer corners. Athena strides left and brandishes her spear with left hand, her shield seems suspended in midair. On side A the shield shows a human leg and thigh, which Jeffrey Hurwit noted was the emblem of a prominent antityrannical family in Athens, and on side B a snake. Athena wears high-crested Athenian helmet and peplos incised with stars. Behind her Hermes walks right but turns back. A warrior, wearing Corinthian helmet, thorax, greaves, and chitoniskos (short dress worn by both sexes) is accompanied by child, and both supplicate the goddess. Yale curator Susan Matheson, in a letter to W. G. Moon in 1984, identified this as an Ajax and Kassandra scene. According to Matheson, "The miniature figure of Kassandra taking refuge at Athena's feet [on side A] (even hiding her head behind the shield with snakes on side B), running towards Athena while looking back at Ajax, dressed in a short chiton and chlamys, all occur on various black-figure versions as illustrated in the LIMC. The confrontation of a left-facing Athena with raised spear with the right-facing Ajax (usually armed with a sword, but isn't he holding one in his right hand on side A?) is standard in black-figure as well. Ajax's raised hand appears on British Museum B242 (LIMC Aias II 34), and Hermes appears as an 'extra' in LIMC #24 and #33a. There do not, from the LIMC lists at least, appear to be any other examples of cups with the scene on the outside, but, as with Yale's unique red-figure plate, that should hardly preclude the identification." Gloria Ferrari Pinney echoed this identification in her review in AJA 85 (1981): 503–4, of *Greek Vase-Painting in Midwestern Collections*.

Red is added to the perimeter of shields and second ring and centers of eyes, stripe on wreathes of both helmets and for brim of Hermes' hat, Hermes' beard, and stripes on chlamys. White is added to shield devices outer eye, dots on warriors' crest-bands; on side A only minuscule dots on Hermes' belt and in a band around Hermes' neck, on warrior's right hand; on side B only the crown of Hermes' traveling hat. The tondo has a gorgon head with red added to alternating rolls of hair on forehead, tongue.

Bibliography: Moon, *Greek Vase-Painting in Midwestern Collections*, 102–3, cat. no 59. Elvehjem *Bulletin* (1985–86): 51 (illus.).

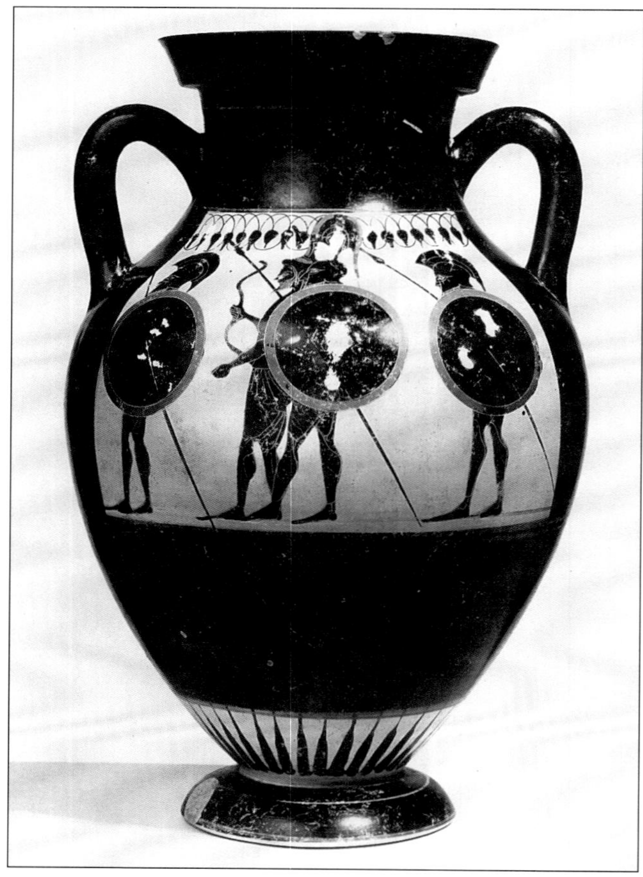

Side B

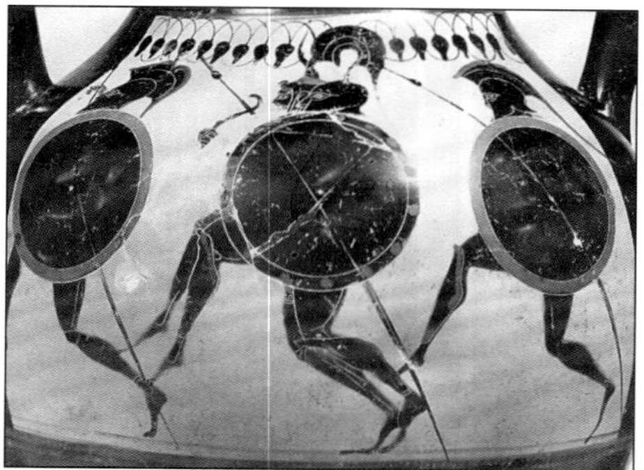

Detail of side A

31
Attic Black-figure Amphora (Type B)
Circle of the Antimenes Painter (Attribution by W. G. Moon)
Ca. 520–510 B.C.
H. 15 1/2 in. 39.4 cm; d. with handles 9 1/2 in. 24.1 cm; d. of belly 10 in. 25.4 cm; d. rim 6 11/16 in. 17 cm; d. foot 5 3/8 in. 13.7 cm
Hilldale Fund purchase, 63.10.2, K. J. Hewett, London, Sotheby's

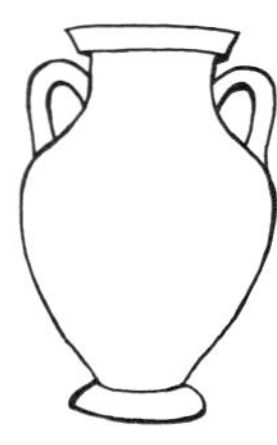

Condition: Mostly intact and fine state of preservation except for large chip on the boot, smaller chips on rim and handles, some repaired cracks and restored areas on main panel.

Decoration: Amphora has flaring lip, echinus foot, and ear-shaped handles. Inside the neck the black glaze descends to a depth of 1 5/8 inches; the top of the rim is reserved showing the natural orange color of the clay, as is the underside of the base. A lotus-bud frieze is at the top of the panels. Side A in reserved panel has three running hoplites accompanied by a Sythian bowman armed with spears and shields in the following designs: (left-right) three balls, a leg, chariot's car. Side B has same three hoplites and bowman walking with these shield designs: (left-right) a leg, boucraneon, three balls. Bottom of belly has zone of rays.

Bibliography: W. G. Moon, "Two Vases in the Circle of the Antimenes Painter," Elvehjem *Bulletin* (1974–75): n.p.

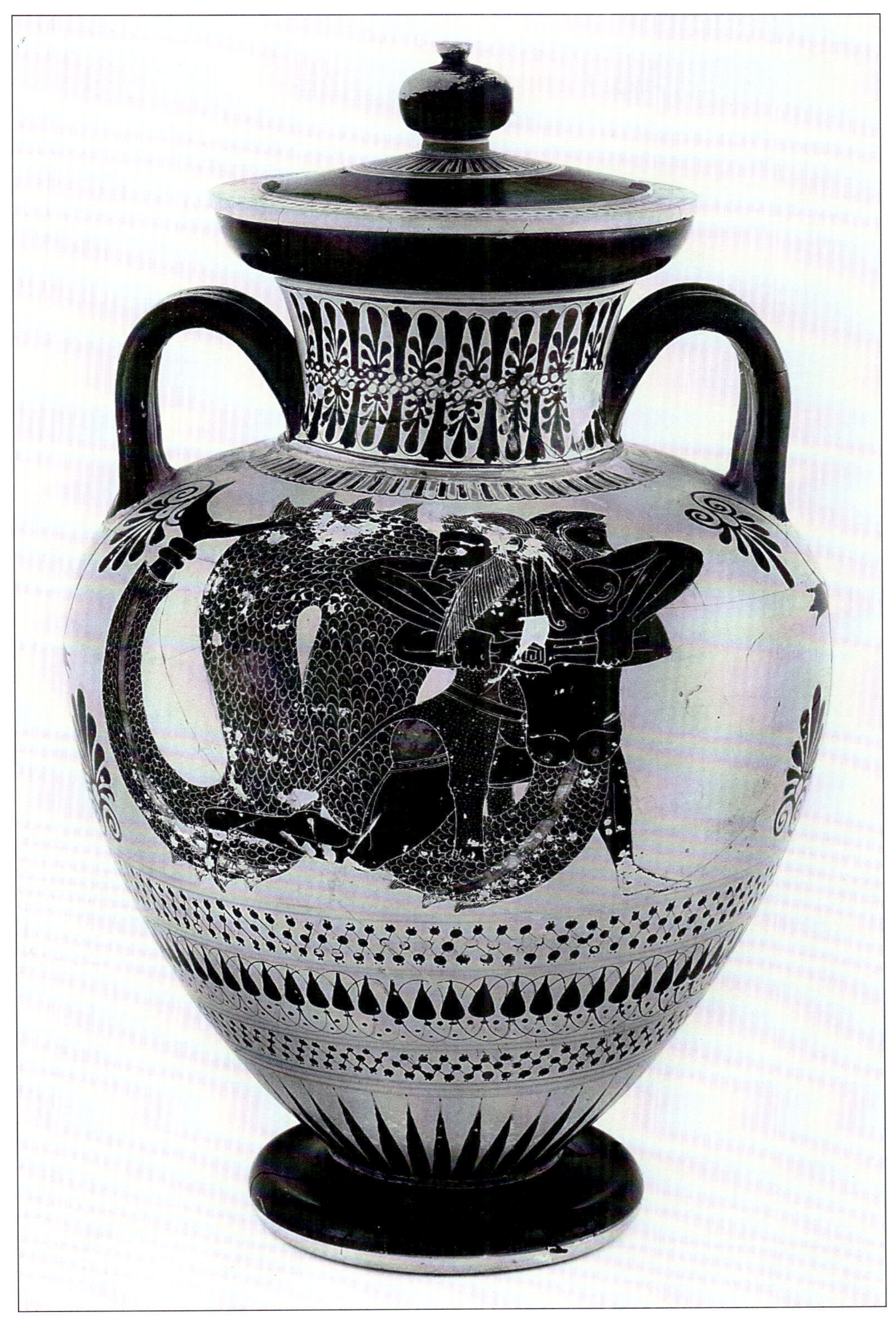

32 Side B

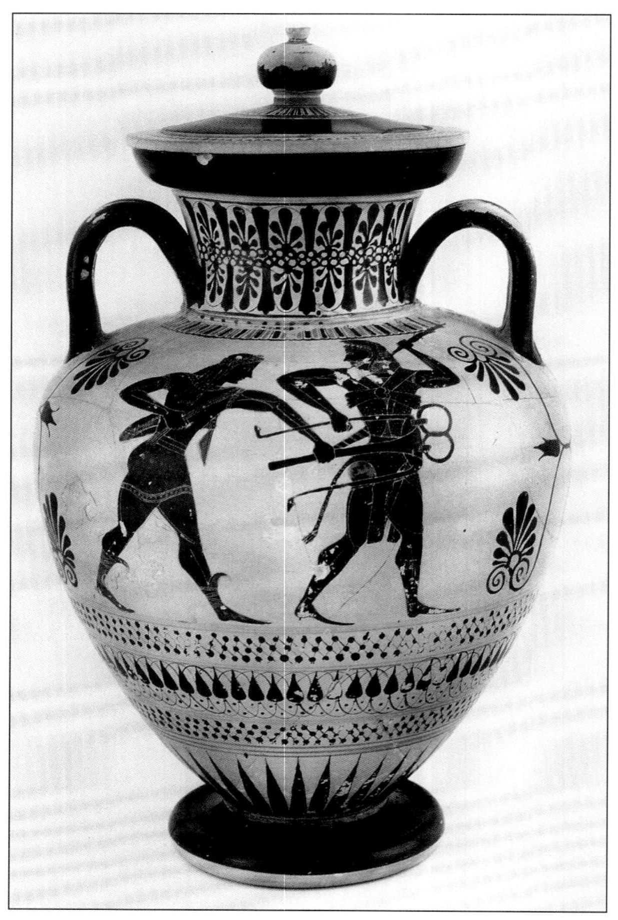

Side A

32

Attic Black-figure Neck-amphora

Possibly Chiusi Painter (attribution by W. G. Moon)

Ca. 520–500 B.C.

H. with lid 20 9/16 in. 52.2 cm; h. without lid 17 13/16 in. 45.2 cm; d. of spout 10 1/4 in. 26 cm; d. foot 6 9/16 in. 6.7 cm

Tenth Anniversary Fund, Elvehjem Endowment Fund, and Art Collections Fund purchase, 1983.6, Gianfranco Becchina, Antike Kunst Palladion, Basel, Switzerland; Karl Haug collection (from 1935), Basel

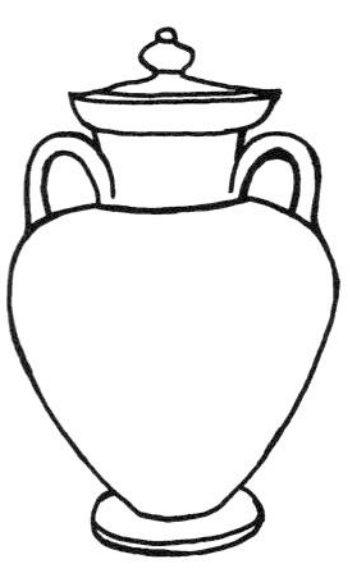

Condition: Complete, no overpainting but broken and mended from large fragments. Holes in the neck remain from ancient repair.

Decoration: Around the neck is a lotus and palmette chain in silhouette; on the shoulder, a pattern of alternate red and black tongues. On side A Herakles fights Apollo for the Delphic tripod; on side B Herakles fights Triton. Beneath handle is a pattern of four palmettes connected by a tendril with lotus bud in center. These palmettes effectively frame the scenes on both sides A and B. Below figural scene are two bands of linked balls on either side of a chain of upright lotus buds with dots below, separated by three narrow lines from a ray pattern at base. Incised lines indicate scales of Triton and outline figures, their beards and muscles. The lid is decorated by knob handles surrounded by tongue design and glazed band outlined by ivy pattern.

In 1982 W. G. Moon, professor of art history at the University of Wisconsin–Madison, declared, this "amphora is the equal of the painter's name vase in the Chiusi Musum (1812, ABV, p. 389 middle and Paralipomena p. 171)." Dietrich von Bothmer, Metropolitan Museum in New York, in a letter of February 1983, declined to endorse the attribution to the Chiusi Painter, "the Triton side, in particular, is rather different from *Para* p. 171, 8–10."

Bibliography: Elvehjem *Bulletin* (1981–83): 87 (illus.).

33
Attic Black-figure Kyathos
The Nikosthenic Workshop
Ca. 515 B.C.
H. with handle and spur 5 3/4 in. 14.7 cm; h. to lip of cup 3 1/4 in. 8 cm; d. 4 1/2 in. 11.3 cm; d. foot 2 /12 in. 6.4 cm
Gift of Warren E. Gilson, 1986.50, Lincoln Higgie, Chicago

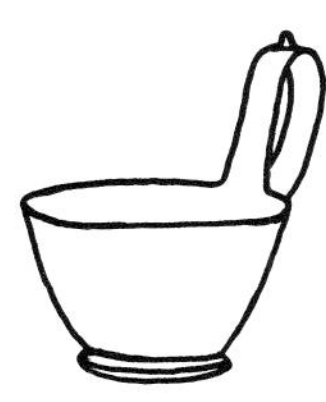

Condition: Surface has suffered from incrustation and part of the scene has flaked off the surface around the lip, right side, interior, and handle. Vase is complete.

Decoration: Dionysos reclines on a pallet and is approached by dancing satyr from left and dancing maenad from right. Behind Dionysos is large vine with triangular-shaped leaves that gives background to scene. On both sides of scene is large "male" eye and vine spray. Red is added to fine wreath in Dionysos' hair, his beard, and stripes on the himation; on the satyr's hair, beard, tail; dots on the maenad's garment; concentric band on "eyes." White added on god's himation, maenad's flesh, and dots on garment, and outer ones of "eyes." Eisman suggests that the pedestrian maenad is painted by a different hand than the vigorous figues of Dionysos and the satyr.

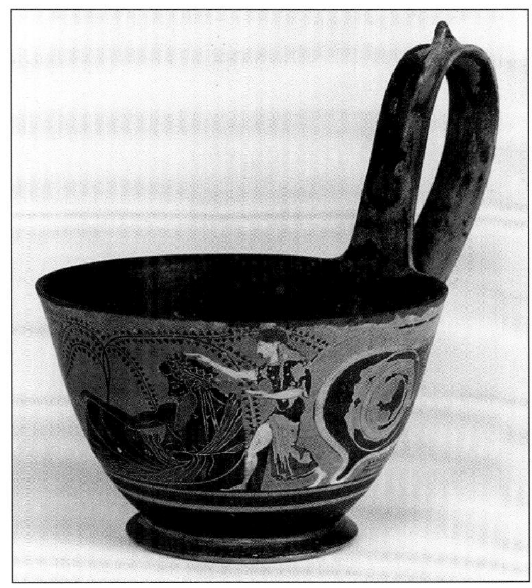

Production of this small, single-handled dipping cup is mostly confined to the Nikosthenic workshop, made between 535 and 485 B.C. It was designed after Etruscan prototypes for export to Etruria. About 450 examples are known. On this vase there are no figures between the large eyes and the handle; the heads of Dionysos and the satyr are too large for their bodies. The incision of the satyr and Dionysos, particularly the rib cage and the stomach muscles, says M. M. Eisman, shows influence of red-figure styles of 520–510, B.C. and allows secure dating for this cup.

Bibliography: Michael M. Eisman (Temple University), in Moon, *Greek Vase-Painting in Midwestern Collections*, 123, cat. no. 69. Elvehjem *Bulletin* (1986–87): 74 (illus.). For background and other examples, see M. M. Eisman, "Attic Kyathos Production," *Archaeology* 28 (1975): 76–83.

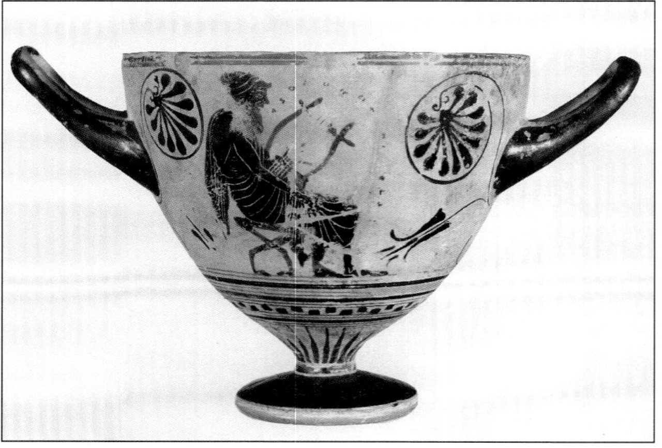

34
Attic White-ground Footed Mastoid-skyphos
Pistias Class "M" (Attribution by D. C. Kurtz)
Ca. 515 B.C.
H. 4 9/16 in. 11.5 cm; d. with handles 12 1/2 in. 31.7 cm; d. without handles 7 5/8 in. 19.4 cm; d. foot 2 3/8 in. 6 cm
Winston Cyril Nave Fund purchase, 1979.122, Bruce and Ingrid McAlpine, London; Collection von Sodenstern, Germany

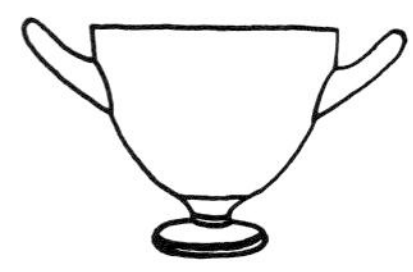

Condition: Recomposed from several fragments. Small patch in plaster under handles, scuffing of white ground and glaze loss from palmettes, figures, and handles; chips on handles and other surface abrasions.

Decoration: Interior of the vase is completely glazed; insides of handles, edges, and underside of foot reserved. Raised fillet painted red marks junction of foot with body. Pairs of dilute lines around the lip, beneath the figures, and alternating with a single, darker glaze line to the zone of rays. A fine band of billet-design is above rays. Palmettes beneath handles have thin tendril that connects to and encircles palmette above handles. Similar on both sides, a poet dressed in himation with hair in a sakkos plays the cithara and sings. His song spills from his mouth in words that seem meaningless.

Bibliography: ABV, 627 "M" for attribution by Donna Kurtz. Moon, *Greek Vase-Painting in Midwestern Collections*, 123, cat. no. 70. Ian Morris and Barry Powell, eds. A *New Companion to Homer* (Leiden 1997), cover illus. Elvehjem *Bulletin* (1978–80): 83 (illus.).

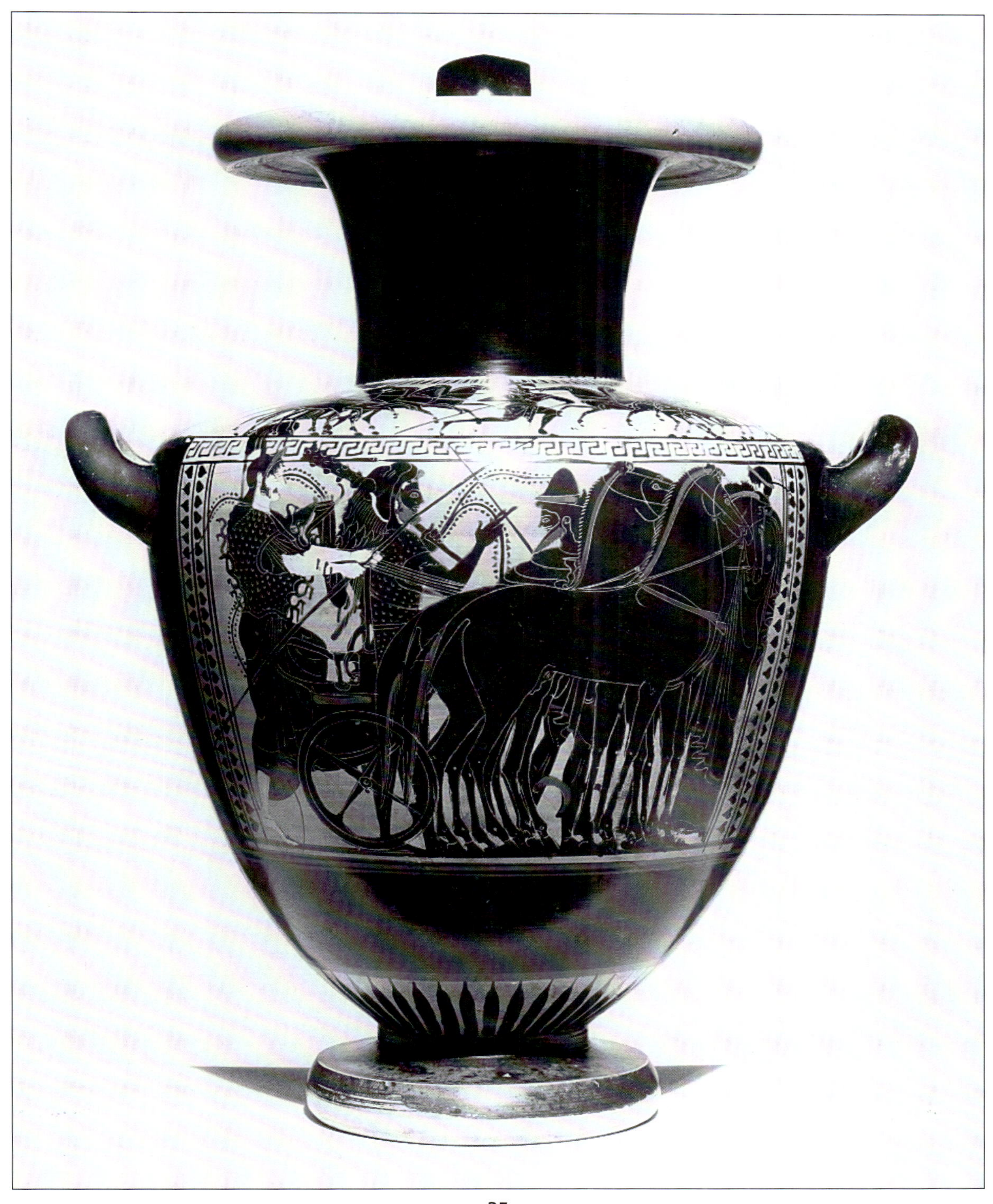

35

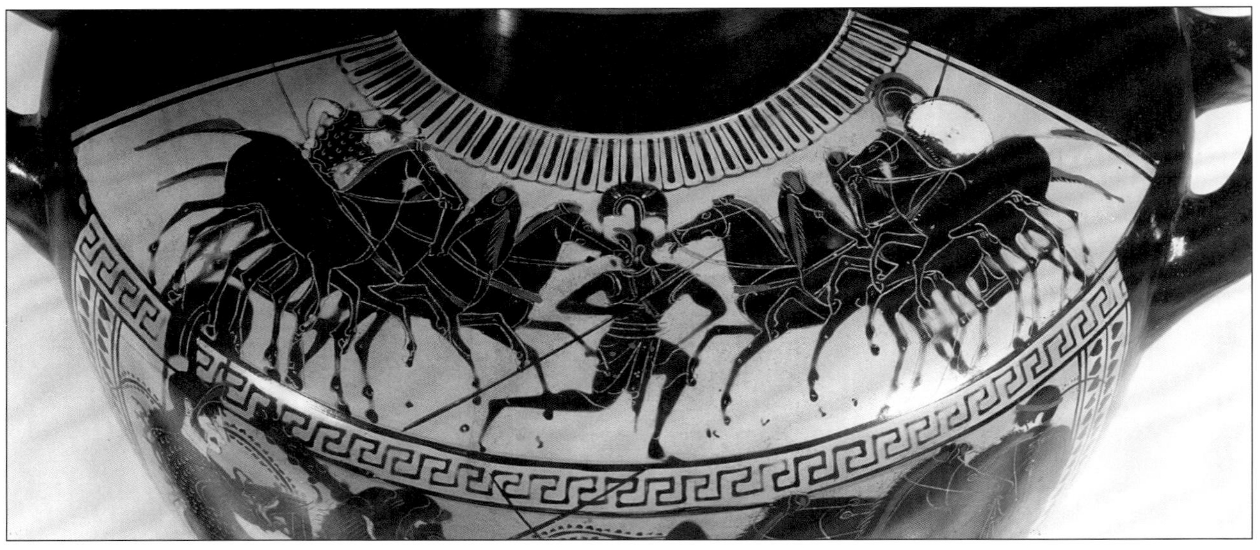

35

Attic Black-figure Hydria

Priam Painter, Potter of the Heavy Hydrai, late 6th century B.C.

(Attribution by J. D. Beazley)

Ca. 510 B.C.

H. 21 1/4 in. 54 cm; h. to lip 19 1/16 in. 48.5 cm; w. 15 3/4 in. 40.1 cm; d. of mouth 10 1/2 in. 26.7 cm; d. of base in. 6 5/8 in. 16.9 cm

Gift of Mr. and Mrs. Arthur J. Frank, 68.14.1, Munzen und Medaillen, A.G., Basel, Switzerland

Condition: Excellent condition, mended from a few large pieces; complete with no restorations.

Decoration: Main panel shows the departure of Herakles for Olympos. Athena, on far left steps into chariot, which will take Herakles to his reward of immortality on sacred mount. Athena wears aegis, high-crested Athenian helmet and holds a kentron or goad in right hand. Herakles, with quiver of arrows on back, club in left hand, and lion-scalp on head, gestures to Hermes who will guide the journey. Hermes wears chlamys or cloak, chiton, winged boots, and petasos or traveling hat and also carries goad. A female attendant quiets the team of horses. At the bottom of the scene is an inscription: |V|OSK|A|Λ|O|S

On the shoulder, a fully armed Athena in added white, on the left, mounts a chariot that is depicted in three-quarter view; a similiar chariot is driven by a male (Ares?) in Corinthian panoply. Both chariots converge on a fleeing giant (Enkelados?). Separating main panel and shoulder scene are meanders; bands of ivy frame the panel on either side; a zone of alternating red and black tongues is above the shoulder scene; a zone of rays arises from the foot. Above the main panel are meanders to the right and bands of ivy on either side. Two red lines run completely around the vase beneath the main picture, another is above the zone of rays, and the rotelles on either side of the pouring handle are red. Graffito on the underside of base.

Bibliography: Munzen und Medaillen, *Kunstwerke der Antike*, Auktion 26 (October 5, 1963), 57, cat. no. 100, illus. p. 35. Beazley, *Para.*, 146–47, no. 26 bis. Elvehjem *Bulletin* (1970–71): 43 (illus.). W. G. Moon, "Two Vases in the Circle of the Antimenes Painter," Elvehjem *Bulletin* (1974–75): n.p. Moon, *Greek Vase-Painting in Midwestern Collections*,116–17, cat. no. 66. Moon, "The Priam Painter: Some Iconographic and Stylistic Considerations," in *Ancient Greek Art and Iconography* ed. W. G. Moon (Madison 1983), 97–118, illus. 99. *Murlo and the Etruscans:Art and Society in Ancient Etruria*, ed. Richard Daniel DePuma and Jocelyn Penny Small (Madison 1994), 107, illus. 109.

36

Attic Red-figure Lekythos

The Painter of Palermo 4 (Attribution by J. D. Beazley, formerly attributed to Pan Painter)

Ca. 480–470 B.C.

H. 11 7/16 in. 29 cm; d. at shoulder 3 1/2 in. 9 cm; d. rim 2 1/8 in. 5.4 cm; d. foot 2 11/16 in. 6.8 cm

Gift of Mr. and Mrs. Arthur J. Frank, 1976.143, Ars Antiqua, AG, Lucern, Switzerland

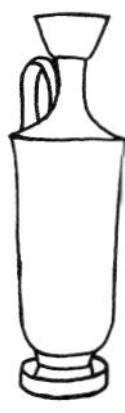

Condition: Intact; brush marks and slight streaking of glaze, misfiring on reverse of body and foot; minor pitting and flaking under handle.

Decoration: The scene is Nike holding fillet. A winged female figure strides right, carrying a fillet in outstretched arms. The wings of the female extend onto the shoulder of the lekythos. The figure is positioned on a groundline composed of an uneven arrangement of pairs of stopped meander-patterns separated by single cross-square. A thin band of close vertical strokes, with a reserved line above, accentuates the flare at the base of the neck. The figure wears an Ionic chiton and short himation; the right sleeve is decorated with rows of crosses between groups of pleats; the hem is bordered with a band of dots. The tops of the wings are dotted. Around her right arm is a spiral bracelet. The figure's hands are reversed.

Bibliography: Ars Antiqua AG, *Kunstwerke der Antike* (June 1966), cat. no. 77, illus. Pl. 14. Beazley, *Para.*, 358, no. 4 bis. Harvey Sweet, "A Greek Lekythos and a Roman Season Sarcophagus in the Elvehjem Art Center," Ph.D. diss. University of Wisconsin–Madison, 1972. Moon, *Greek Vase-Painting in Midwestern Collections*, 102, cat. no. 59; see page 102 for argument on attribution.

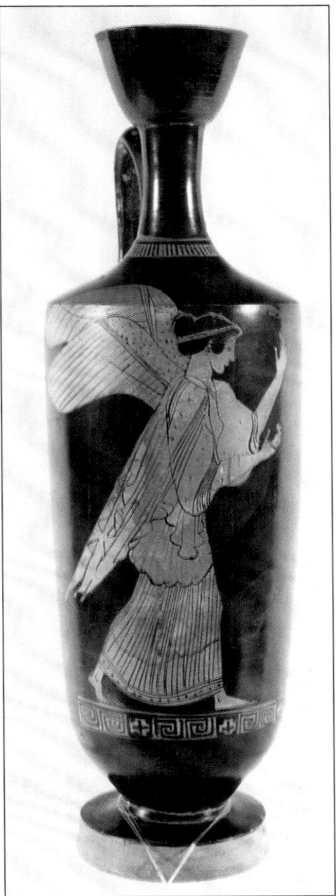

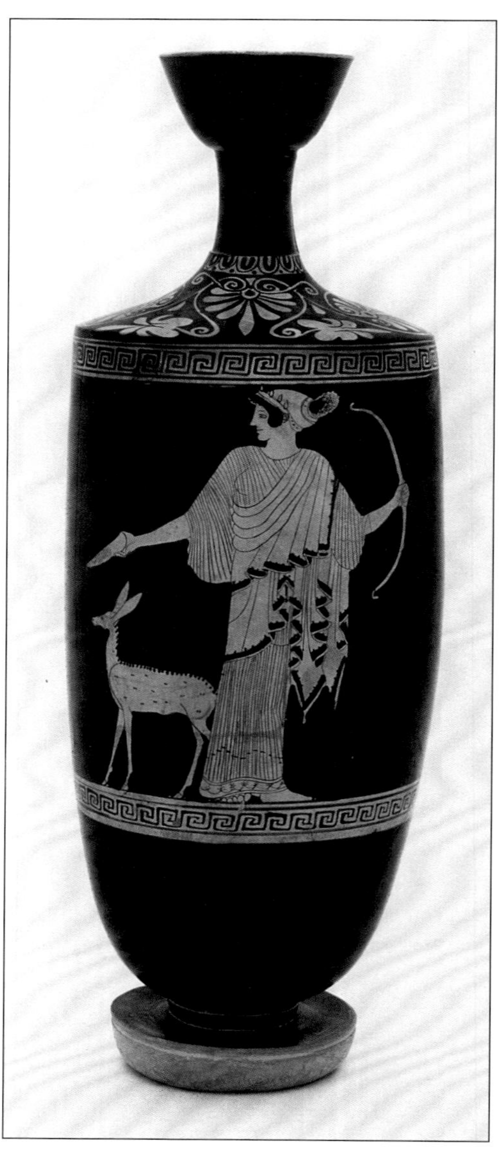

37
Attic Red-figure Lekythos
Oreithia Painter (active 2nd quarter of 5th century B.C.)
(Attribution by Herbert A. Cahn, 1970)
Ca. 470 B.C.
H. 17 11/16 in. 45 cm; d. rim 3 1/8 in. 8 cm; d. 6 in. 15.2 cm; d. foot 3 7/8 in. 9.6 cm
Gift of Mr. and Mrs. Arthur J. Frank, 1985.93, Munzen und Medaillen AG, Basel, Switzerland

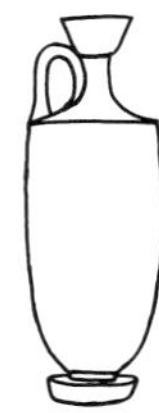

Condition: Reassembled. Glaze abraded and small areas of chipping throughout. Patches of discoloration, abrasion near head and feet of figure and on handle. Base of foot highly abraded, glaze chipped.

Decoration: Artemis stands with body front, head in profile facing left. In her left hand she holds a phiale (vessel); in her right she holds a bow. She wears chiton and himation banded in black with dots. The hem of the chiton is banded with delicate floral chain. Her hair is in a kekryphalos, a cloth for binding the hair with a stephane (wreath) over. Beside her is a spotted doe in profile facing left. At the bottom of the neck is egg-and-dot border; the shoulder is decorated with a chain of palmettes. A border of menanders frames the figural scene above and below.

Bibliography: Munzen und Medaillen AG, *Kunstwerke der Antike* Auktion 40 (December 1969), cat. no. 99. Hans Walter, *Griechishe Gotter* (Munich 1971), 203–4, fig. 180. Lilly Kahil, *Lexicon Iconographicum Mythologiae Classicae*, vol. 2 (Zurich 1984), 695, no. 970, pl. 517. For Oreithyia Painter, J. D. Beazley, *Attic Red-Figure Vase-Painters* (Oxford 1942), 496–97.

38
Attic Red-figure Lekythos
Aischines Painter (Attribution by J.D. Beazley)
Ca. 470 B.C.
H. 7 7/8 in. 20 cm; d. rim 1 3/8 in. 3 cm; d. 2 1/2 in. 6.4 cm; d. foot 1 13/16 in. 4.5 cm
Gift of Herbert M. Howe, 1978.1178, K. Adam, Athens, Greece, 1936

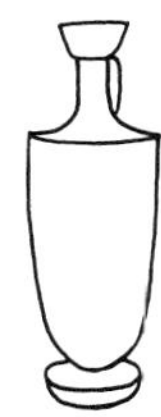

Condition: Intact. Heavily abraded with flaking black on main panel, handle, and foot.

Decoration: The neck is reserved; the shoulder is separated with short vertical strokes and evenly spaced simple palmettes. Nike flies to the right, holding a wreath or sash and wearing himation, chiton, and sakkos. At top of figural scene is meander border; below scene is uneven reserved line.

Bibliography: ARV, 709, no. 2. Elvehjem *Bulletin* (1985–86): 50 (illus.).

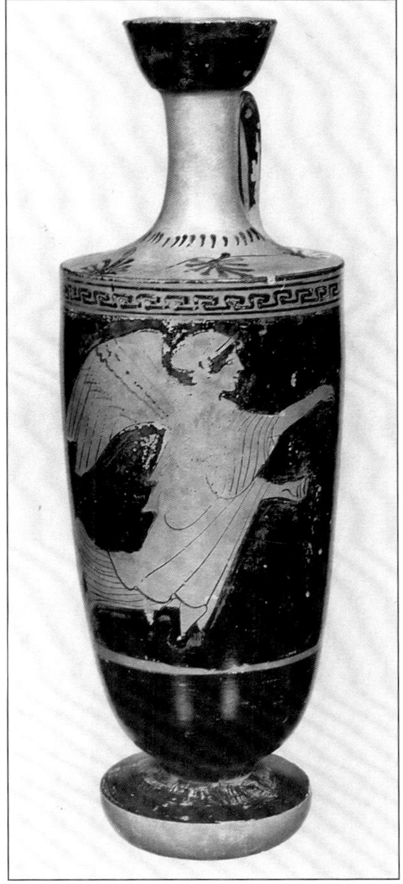

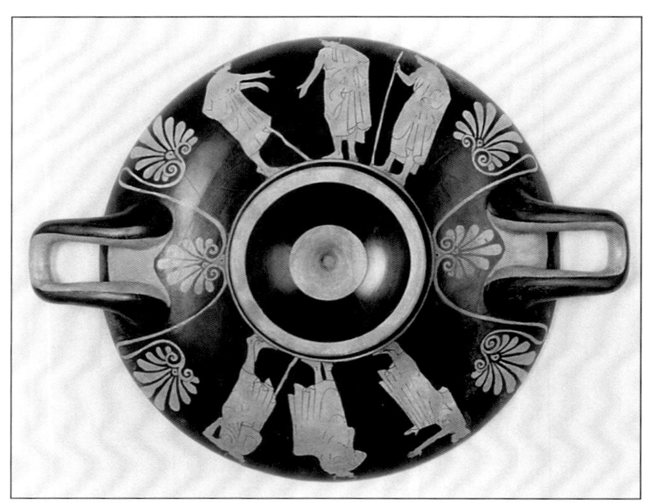

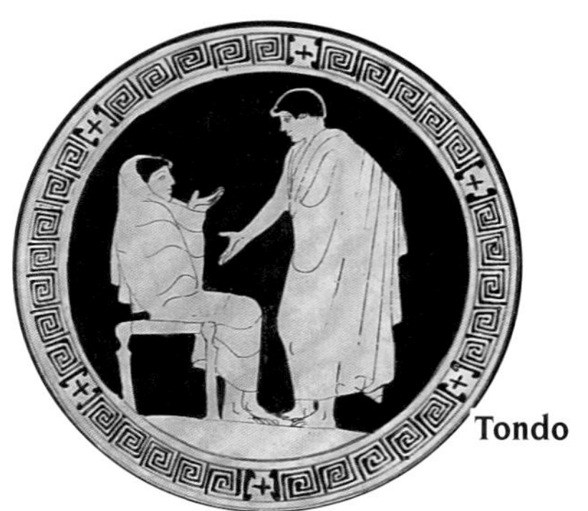

Tondo

39
Attic Red-figure Kylix
Akestorides Painter, Workshop of Douris (active 2nd quarter of 5th century B.C.) (Attribution by Herbert A. Cahn)
Ca. 460 B.C.
H. 3 3/4 in. 9.5 cm; d. with handles 12 3/16 in. 31 cm; d. without handles: 9 3/8 in. 23.8 cm; d. foot 3 3/4 in. 9.5 cm
Gift of Mr. and Mrs. Arthur J. Frank, 1985.94, Robert J. Myers, New York, N.Y., Joel L. Malter & Co., Encino, Cal.

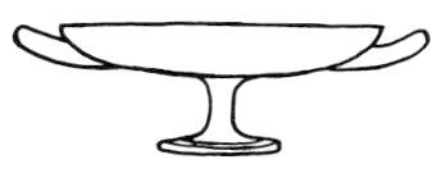

Condition: Reassembled and repainted along seams of fragments and on side B near head of figure. Red abraded and uneven density.

Description: Interior roundel depicts two youths, one standing, the other seated, in animated conversation. Exterior of both sides shows three youths in conversation framed by one palmette at side and one beneath each handle, connected by tendril.

Gisela Richter, in *Red-Figured Athenian Vases in the Metropolitan Museum of Art* (New Haven 1936) writes of the artist, "The style of the Askestorides Painter is related to that of the Painter of Munich 2660 as well as that of the early Euaion Painter, but his works have a delicacy of feeling not attained by either of those artists" (pp. 137, 138). He is named after an inscription on New York 22.139.72 from Aegina.

Bibliography: *Journal of Numismatic Fine Arts* 2.2 (Summer 1973), cover illustration. For Akestorides Painter, Workshop of Douris, J. D. Beazley, *Attic Red-Figure Vase-Painters*, 2nd ed.(Oxford 1963, 781.

40
Attic White-ground Lekythos
Near the Timokrates Painter (Attribution by W. G. Moon, formerly the Timocrates Painter, attribution by H. A. Cahn)
Ca. 460 B.C.
H. 15 7/8 in. 40.3 cm; d. rim 3 1/4 in. 8.2 cm; d. at shoulder 5 1/4 in. 13.3 cm; d. foot 3 1/4 in. 8.2 cm
Edna G. Dyar Fund and Fairchild Foundation Fund purchase, 70.2, Munzen und Medaillen, AG Basel, Switzerland, unknown private Basel or English collection

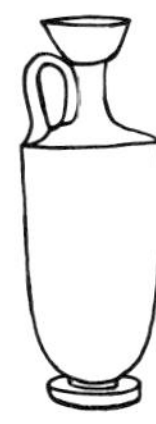

Condition: Broken and repaired, minor strengthening of a few glaze lines and slight retouching of second white, especially on left foot of matron and right foot of handmaiden. Black is dilute and misfired in various places on the vase-body.

Decoration: Women on way to cemetery carry baskets of funerary gifts, fillets, ribbons, and lekythoi; one partly frontal matron wears a black mourning cloak over a red-brown peplos, while the other, possibly her maid, is dressed in yellow-brown Doric peplos fastened at the shoulder with an elaborate pin. The older has a diadem in her hair, the maid wears a fillet and possibly more jewelry as indicated by a row of black dots above this fillet. Each woman carries a basket painted to match the other's clothing. The black basket and ribbons are decorated with a series of black dots, the lighter basket with brown, woven meander-patterns and the ribbons with zigzag designs or speckles.
The horizontal inscription in slip between two women's heads reads "Kalos" (handsome); the vertical inscription in slip between two figures "Glaukon" (name). On shoulder palmettes linked by tendrils below an egg-and-dot band. Above and below the scene is a meander with crossed squares. The underside of foot is reserved and shows graffiti.

Bibliography: H. A. Cahn, *Kunstwerke der Antike*, Munzen und Medaillen Auktion 40 (December 13, 1969), 68, lot 111, illus. pls. 47–48. Elvehjem *Bulletin* (1970–71): 44 (illus.). D. C. Kurtz, *Athenian White Lekythoi: Patterns and Painters* (Oxford 1975), 27, 45, 206, pl. 25.3 and frontispiece. W. Biers, *Outline of Greek Archaeology* (Cornell 1979), illus. fig. 8.60. Moon *Greek Vase-Painting in Midwestern Collections*, 192, cat. no. 107. Christine M. Havelock, "Mourners on Greek Vases: Remarks on the Social History of Women," in *The Greek Vase* ed. Stephen L. Hyatt (Troy, N.Y. 1981), 115, pl. 93.

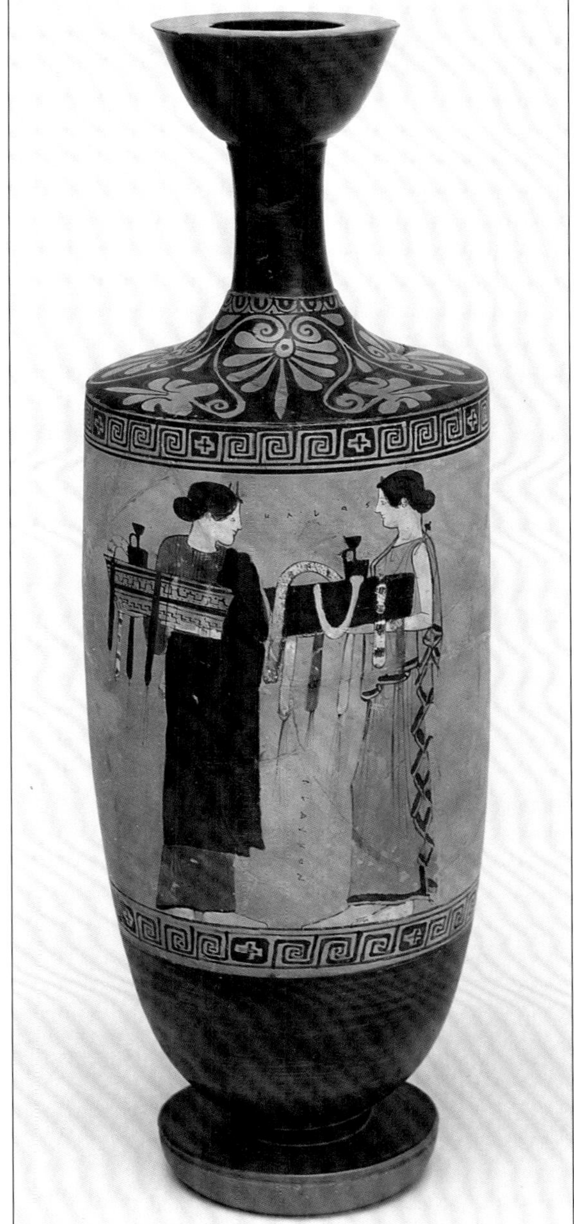

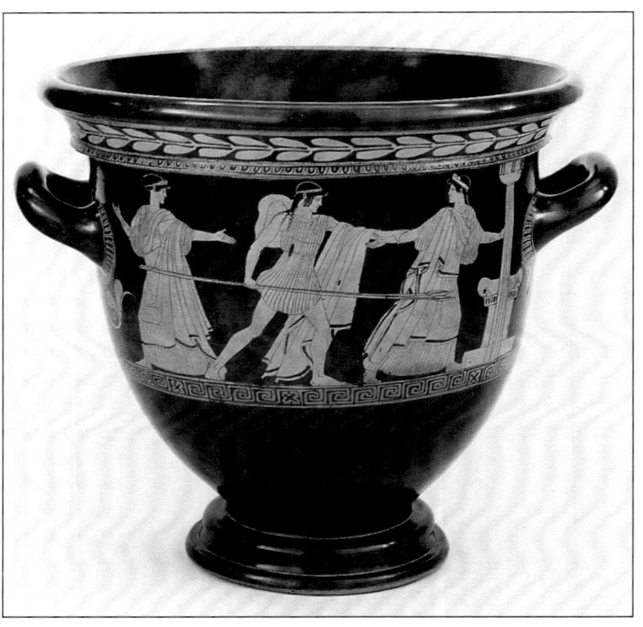

Side A

41
Attic Red-figure Bell Krater
Follower of Niobid Painter (Attribution by J. D. Beazley)
Ca. 460–450 B.C.
H. 14 in. 35.5 cm; d. with handles 17 in. 43.2 cm; d. without handles 15 3/4 in. 40 cm; d. foot 7 1/4 in. 18.4 cm
Gift of Mr. and Mrs. Arthur J. Frank, 69.31.1, Andre Emmerich Gallery, Inc., New York, N.Y.

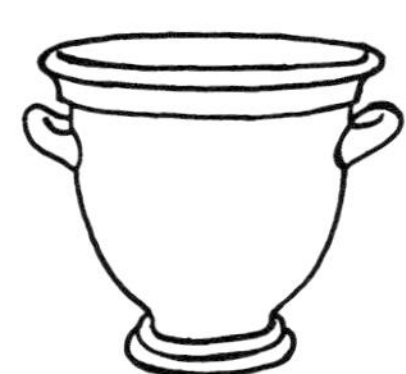

Condition: Intact. Surface abraded. Side B shows speckles of dark pigment throughout red.

Decoration: Double-curved foot, each curve offset by a narrow reserved line. Below the rim olive-wreath and egg pattern, palmettes in the handle area with handles encircled by tongue pattern. Side A shows Theseus pursuing Helen. The scene occurs within a sanctuary indicated by an altar appearing behind a slender Doric column. Helen is fleeing towards it. Grasping the column with her left hand, she looks back at her pursuer who has seized her by the right forearm. On the left, Helen's female companion hurries away, reaching out towards her mistress with a gesture of bewildered indecision. Both women wear chitons and himatia with double border, coronets in their hair. Theseus appears as traveler with short chiton and petasos. He carries two long spears in right hand. Side B shows a maid bringing the news to a queen. A Doric column suggests the interior of the palace. In front of it stands the queen, distinguished by coronet and scepter. A woman hurries towards her, gesticulating. Behind the column another woman of rank rushes up to listen. The pursuit of women by gods and heroes, and particularly by the Attic national hero Theseus, becomes a favorite subject of red-figured vase painting in the second quarter of the fifth century B.C.

On side A the hands are clearly articulated; on side B hands roughly sketched and lines of clothing less finely drawn. Perhaps side A is the more important side to the painter, or perhaps another hand in the workshop is responsible for side B.

Bibliography: Herbert A. Cahn, *Art of the Ancients: Greeks, Etruscans, and Romans* (New York: Andre Emmerich Gallery, 1968), 29 (illus.). Elvehjem *Bulletin* (1970–71): 43 (illus.).

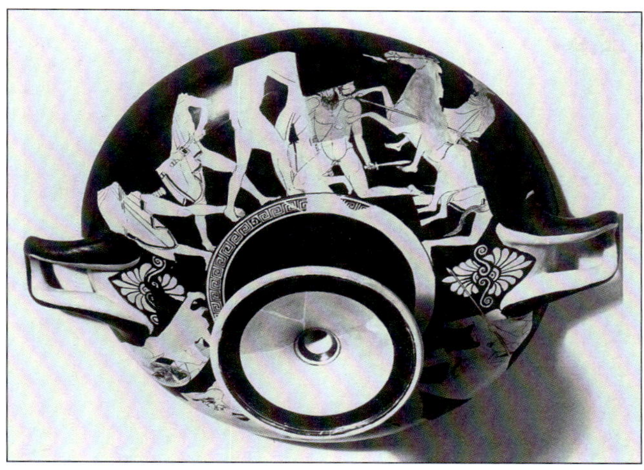

Side A

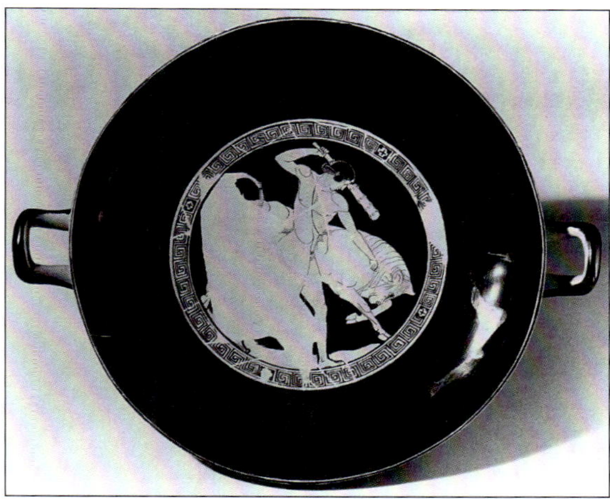

Interior

42
Attic Red-figure Kylix (Type II)
Penthesilea Painter (Attribution by Dietrich von Bothmer)
Ca. 455 B.C.
H. 6 in. 15.3 cm; d. rim 14 5/8 in. 37.1 cm; d. 17 15/16 in. 45.8 cm; d. foot 5 13/16 in. 14.5 cm; h. foot 3 in. 7.7 cm
Gift of Steimke Foundation in memory of W. H. Steimke, 1976.31, Bruce McAlpine, London; private collection, Germany

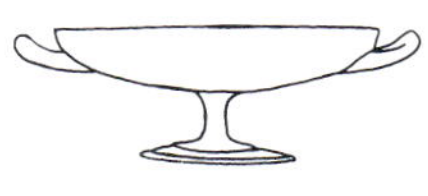

Condition: Assembled from fragments, missing pieces, some large, restored in plaster and painted. Certain fragments discolored under different conditions of preservation; three fragments on the exterior are particularly dark. Interior section of hand end and testicles of bull and lower portion of Theseus' right leg are fragment Louvre CP 11504 (ARV^2,880, no. 14).

Decoration: Interior shows Theseus fighting the bull of Marathon. The tondo is surrounded by a border of meanders, running left, punctuated approximately at the cardinal points, by dotted cross-squares; the cross-square near the bull's head is juxtaposed, mistakenly, onto a meander design. A similar meander pattern borders the exterior pictures below. Exterior side A shows a draped warrior fleeing to the left as a mounted warrior dressed in chlamys and traveling hat, moving to the right, aims a long spear at a fallen kneeling nude figure. The head of the latter, facing right is shown in three-quarter view, his mouth open and teeth exposed. Toward him, a nude compatriot rushes to the left, presumably to protect the fallen man with his shield that shows the device of a snake. The fifth and sixth figures both wear the mantle that is edged with a broad stripe; one warrior with sword drawn pursues the standing nude opponent nearby. Side B shows battle scene arranged in three groups. Nearest left handle a nude warrior moves to the right, long spear in his right hand, shield with apron on his left. His head is protected by a Chalcidian-type helmet, and he fights a pair of warriors, also nude, who face him. One opponent, brandishing a sword, his left side under a shield, has fallen to his knees. He and the mate standing behind, who has come to his aid, also wear the Chalcidian-type helmet; the latter's has a crest and above the visor a floral design. The standing warrior wields a long spear and his shield has a snake emblem. A pair of combatants is next, one draped, one not. The nude man runs to the left, but has turned to parry the attack of the draped warrior who has his sword drawn. The chlamys or mantle has a broad stripe around the edge. The nude warrior's left is protected by a shield with a device of a tripod that has an apron elaborately decorated with bosses and ranks of zigzags. The last pair, near right handle, again has a draped warrior battling one who is nude. The former wears a pilos, a cone-shaped helmet; the latter, as much as is preserved, carries a shield and, in his right hand, a long spear which, running under the handle and through the palmette, leads the viewer to the other side of the vase. Under each handle an arrangement of palmette fans back to back with scroll-tendrils at center.

Bibliography: Moon, *Greek Vase-Painting in Midwestern Collections*, 194–96, cat. no.110. Karl Schefold and Franz Jung, *Die Urkonige, Perseus, Bellerophon, Herakles und Theseus in der klassichen und hellenistichen Kunst* (Munich 1988), 246–47.

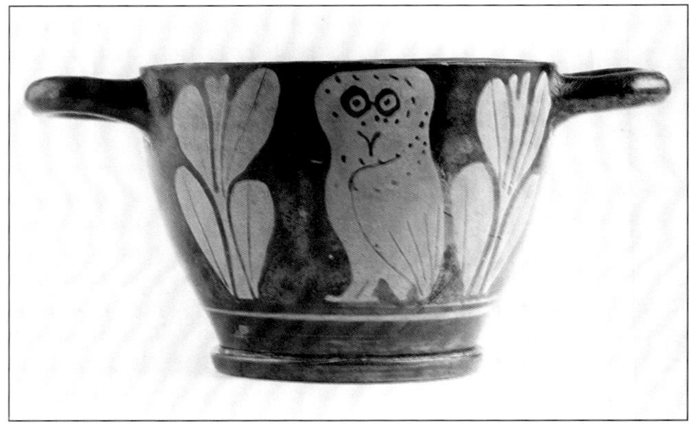

43
Attic Red-figure Owl Skyphos
Ca. 450 B.C.
H. 3 in. 7.2 cm; d. with handles 5 7/8 in. 15 cm; d. without handles 3 11/16 in. 9.4 cm; d. foot 2 7/16 in. 6.2 cm
Gift of Mr. and Mrs. Arthur J. Frank, 1981.131, Hesperia Art, Philadelphia

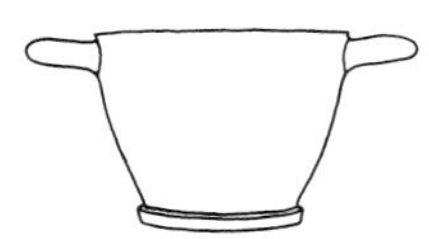

Condition: Intact. Slight chipping of glaze at rim and on foot; some chipping in interior. Black glaze uneven.

Decoration: Sides A and B depict owl standing, body facing left, with face front, and closed wings between two olive sprigs on thin reserved line.

Bibliography: *Hesperia Art Bulletin* 27 (n.d.) cat. no. 11 (illus.).

44
Lucanian Red-figure Kalpis
The Pisticci Painter (Attribution by A. D. Trendell)
Ca. 440–430 B.C.
H. 11 3/16 in. 28.5 cm; d. rim 5 1/8 in. 14 cm; d. with handles 10 1/2 in. 26.7 cm; d. without handles 7 3/4 in. 19.7 cm; d. foot 4 11/16 in. 11.9 cm
Gift of Mr. and Mrs. Arthur J. Frank, 1985.98, The Summa Galleries, Beverly Hills, Cal.

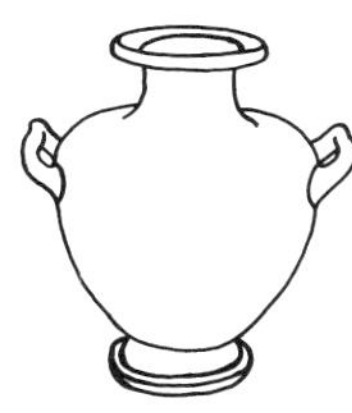

Condition: Intact. Shows tiny areas of chipped glaze at center of painting of three women, undersides of handles (small area around the right handle broken and repaired), and along center rim of foot.

Decoration: On edge of lip is the egg-and-dart pattern, and the base of the neck, only on the front of the vase, has florals. The figured scene is ordered below by a reserve band with black meander interrupted at intervals by saltire squares. The figured scene on the front of the vase shows three women in their quarters, accompanied by a pet heron. The woman in the center carries a mirror in left hand and an alabastron in right; she stands with her body frontal, her head turned to the left, her left foot turned to the right. The other two women stand on either side in profile, facing the center. All three women wear chiton and himatia, the former enhanced in two instances with a fine line somewhat above the hem. The woman on the left wears her hair in a sakkos, or snood; the other two wear head jewelry that may signify special status. The woman at right stoops toward a large kalathos that stands between her and the woman in the center.

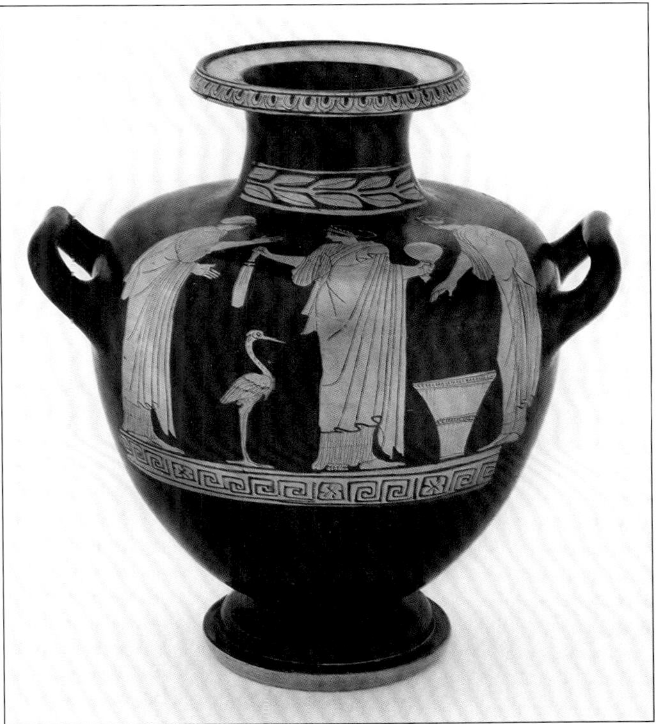

Bibliography: The Summa Galleries, *Ancient Art Catalogue* 5 (September 1979), cat. no. 18. Virginia Museum, *The Art of South Italy: Vases from Magna Graecia* exh. cat.(Richmond 1982), 55, cat. no. 1. A. D. Trendall, *The Red-figured Vases of Lucania, Campania, and Sicily* (London 1983), supplement 3, no. 556.

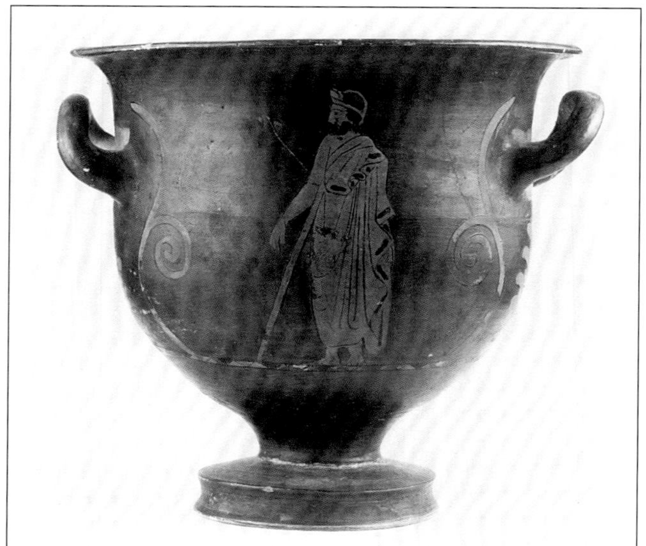

Side A

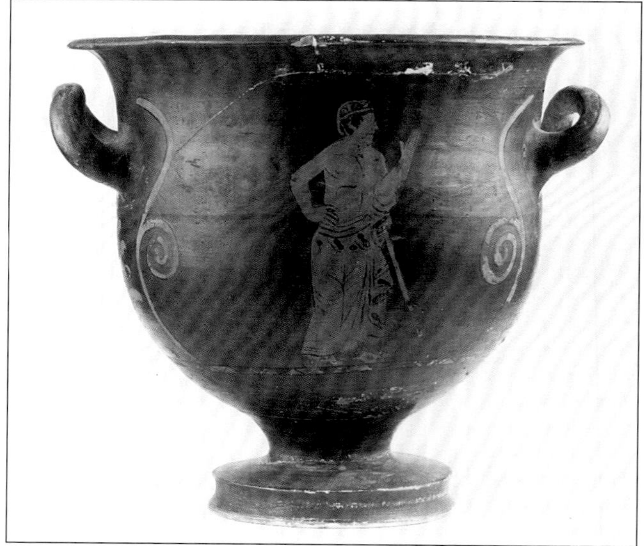

Side B

45
Campanian or Etruscan False Red-figure Bell Krater
4th century B.C.
H. 9 1/4 in. 24 cm; d. 10 in. 25.4 cm
Transfer from UW Department of Classics, 70.18.10.
Purchased for teaching ancient art to classics students, probably in 1920s by Prof. Grant Showerman.

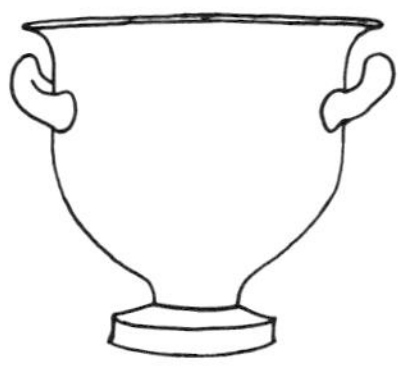

Condition: Not intact. Foot separated from body; reassembled at rim. Soiled and abraded throughout. White plaster visible at foot.

Decoration: Black glaze with added red, detail lines in black slip. Flaring lip, full round body with widest diameter at bottom near foot. Side A shows man standing fully draped in bordered cloak but with bare feet, leaning on a staff that extends from armpit of exposed arm; side B shows beardless youth standing with hand raised, torso bare with musculature detailed in black paint, hair bound by fillet. Waist to ankles covered with draped red cloth with detail in black; bare feet. His staff hangs from bundle at waist, does not reach ground. Both figures are framed by vegetation; beneath is a border that serves as ground line; beneath handles large red palmettes with details in black extending to bottom of unusual red ground line with black traingles applied over red.

Unpublished. Cf. CVA Serres (France 13), Style Apulien, pl. 33, nos. 5, 6, 8, 11–13.

46
Campanian Red-figure Skyphos
4th century B.C.
H. 3 5/8 in. 9.2 cm; d. with handles 5 1/2 in. 14 cm; d. without handles 3 7/16 in. 8.9 cm; d. rim 3 in. 7.6 cm; d. foot 1 5/8 in. 2.9 cm
Transfer from UW Department of Classics, 70.18.6. Purchased for teaching ancient art to classics students, probably in 1920s by Prof. Grant Showerman.

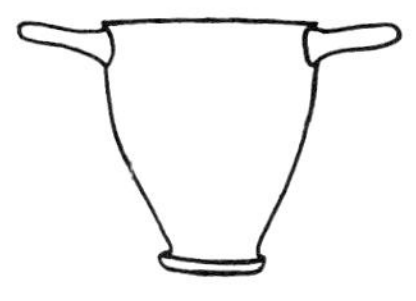

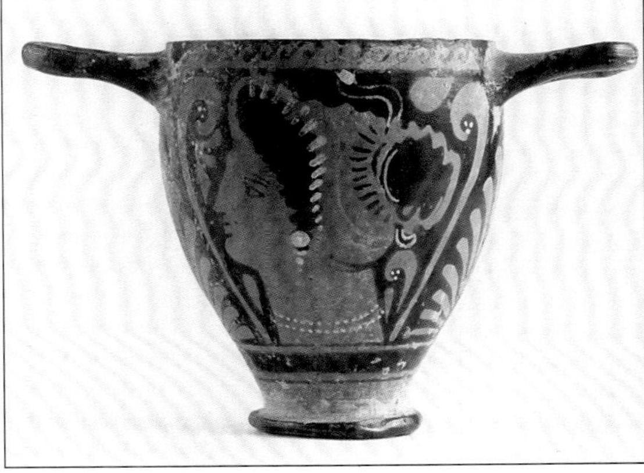

Condition: Intact. Heavily abraded and soiled. Light solid residue covers much of interior and side B. Figure's face on side B shows long triangular area of missing or chipped pigment where not reconstructed in repair.

Decoration: Under each handle a palmette, wave pattern at rim. On both sides profile of woman with added white and yellow for necklace, pendant earrings and on top front of sakkos.

Bibliography: Cf. A.D. Trendall, *The Red-figured Vases of Lucania, Campania and Sicily. Supplement* I (London 1970), 60–61, 195a, 195b, 195c. Cf. CVA Museo de Antichità, Torino I (Italy 32), pl. 22, no. 4, pl. 23, nos. 5,6.

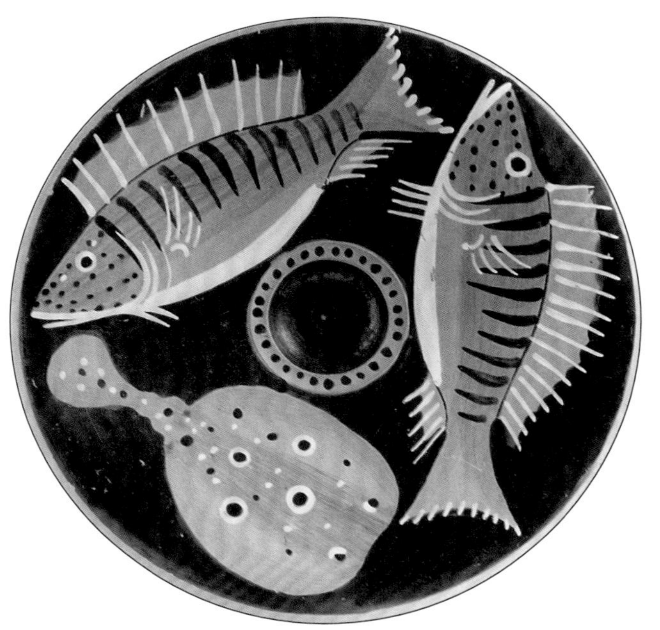

47
Campanian Red-figure Fish Plate
Torpedo Group (Attribution by A.D. Trendall)
Last half of 4th century B.C.
H. 2 in. 5.1 cm; d. 7 1/2 in. 19.1 cm; d. foot 2 15/16 in. 7.4 cm
Gift of Mr. and Mrs. Arthur J. Frank, 1981.132, Hesperia Art, Philadelphia

Condition: Intact. Slight chipping of glaze at top of plate.

Decoration: In interior two perch and a torpedo fish around black central cavity encircled by dots on red band. The gills of the fish consist of three fairly even curves, and the base of the gill fin is placed high and behind the gill. The white understrip of the fish stops just before the tail fin. In the torpedo fish four large spots are carefully edged with white; the oval disc become vestigial, and two small swellings about equal in size come between the fish's body and his paddle-shaped tail. Although there is some debate about the function of these new pottery shapes, one argument has them holding fish offering at graveside rituals. The exterior rim shows running wave pattern, and bottom is decorated with concentric circles.

Bibliography: *Hesperia Art Bulletin* 43,(n.d.), 3, cat. no A20.

48
Campanian Red-figure Skyphos
Frignano Painter (Attribution by A.D. Trendall)
Third quarter of 4th century B.C.
H. 6 1/4 in. 15.9 cm
Transfer from UW Department of Classics, 70.18.13.
Purchased for teaching ancient art to classics students, probably in 1920s by Prof. Grant Showerman.

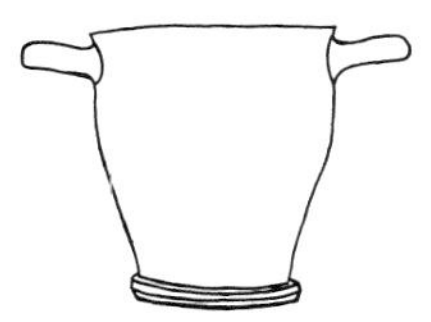

Condition: Intact with hairline cracks around left handle edges. White residue on interior, handles, and foot.

Decoration: The rim is marked by short vertical strokes in added white. Side A shows woman with frontal body and head in profile facing left, holding tambourine. She wears a sakkos and peplos. Side B shows ephebe facing left with white chapelet. Two comma marks to mark the waist of the youth are a signature of the Frignano Painter. White is added to necklace and headdress of woman and to tambourine, to chaplet of youth and to outline the floral and filling decoration. Both figures stand between foliate scrolls, a long vertical leaf that stretches from top to bottom of pot on both sides of the single figure; a single campanula flower blossoms at axial branches of side leaf. The distinctive manner of drawing his floral frames is a clear criterion for attributing the vase to the Frignano Painter. A large palmette is beneath each handle.

Bibliography: A. D. Trendall and Alexander Cambitoglou, *The Red-Figured Vases of Apulia*, vol. 2. Late Apulian (Oxford 1978), 667, no. 208. Emilie Tari, "Some South Italian Vases in the Elvehjem Museum," M.A. Thesis University of Wisconsin, 1975, 41–46. Cf. CVA Museo Campano, Capua 1 (Italy 11), pl. 43, no. 11; Fogg Art Museum 1932.56.39 in *The Art of South Italy; Vases from Magna Graecia*, 203.

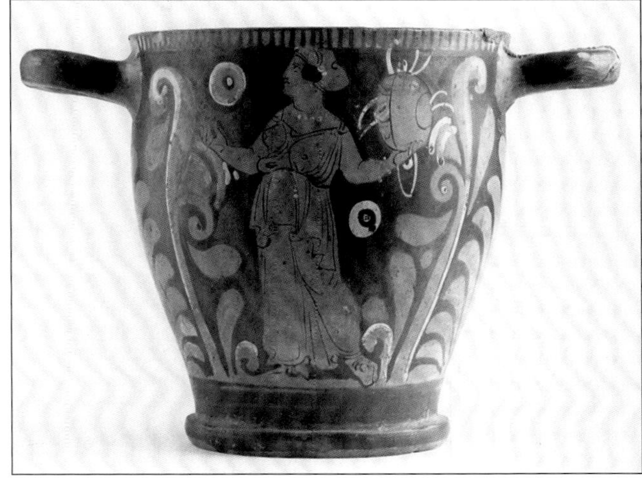

Side A

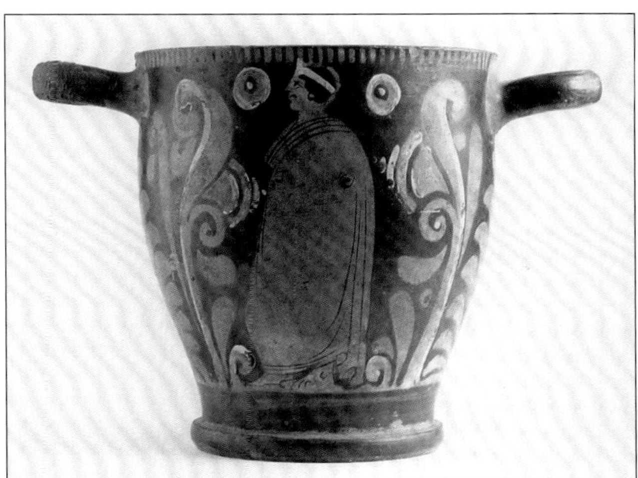

Side B

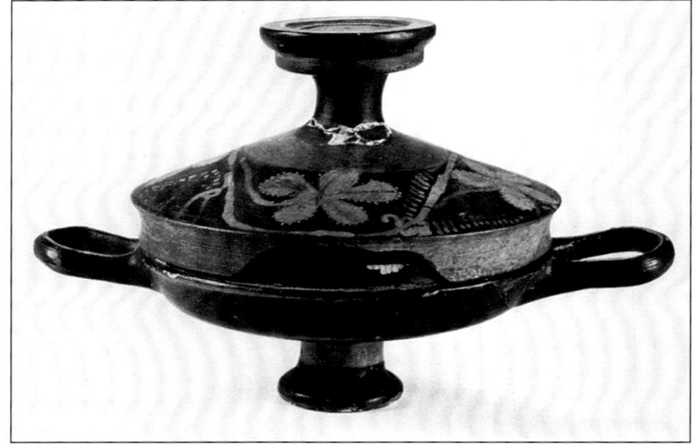

49
Apulian Lekanis with Cover
Ca. 350 B.C.
Body: h. 1 7/8 in. 4.8 cm; d. with handle 6 3/8 in. 16.2 cm; d. without handle 4 1/8 in. 10.5 cm. Lid: h. 2 3/4 in. 7 cm; d. 4 1/8 in. 10.5 cm
Transfer from UW Department of Classics, 70.18.12a-b. Purchased for teaching ancient art to classics students, probably in 1920s by Prof. Grant Showerman.

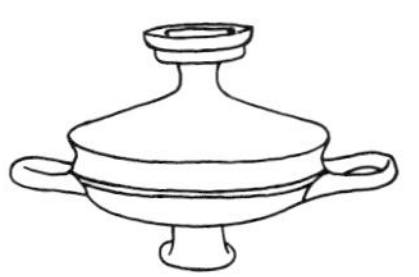

Condition: Intact, but missing chip in foot makes vessel unstable. Reassembled and repainted at seam of fragment on left side near handle. Abrasion on belly caused pigment loss. Lid is missing fragment in base. Neck of handle reassembled with jagged seams and tiny pieces missing.

Decoration: Lid and body are covered in black glaze. The top of disk knob on lid is decorated with radiating black lines. A band of reddish orange is around neck of lid handle. Four white flowers are evenly spaced around top of lid with tendrils connecting them. Yellow and orange stippling is filler between flowers. Lower body is plain black with two horizontal handles. The lower body has a ring of reddish orange around base of stem.

Unpublished. For similar shape, cf. CVA University of Michigan 1(U.S.A. 13), pl. 29, nos. 3 a-b; CVA Museo Provinciale, Lecce 2 (Italy 6), pl. 56, nos. 11–14. For another instance of unusual floral motif on lid, cf. CVA Serres (France 13), pl. 43, no. 34.

50
Apulian Oinochoe
Ca. 350 B.C.
H. 4 1/2 in. 11.5 cm; d. with handles 4 1/8 in. 10.5 cm; d. without handles 3 1/8 in. 7.9 cm; d. foot 2 in. 5.1 cm
Transfer from UW Department of Classics, 70.18.1. Purchased for teaching ancient art to classics students, probably in 1920s by Prof. Grant Showerman.

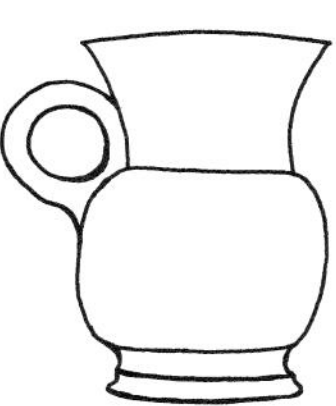

Condition: Intact. Small chips in surface at rim, belly, and left of handle. Solidified residue on neck, interior of rim, and at foot.

Decoration: Black glaze covers surface with the exception of a reserved band of red orange around foot. Thin conical neck with slightly flaring lip decorated by added red and white in a central band: white dots both above and below central red stripe; loop/ring handle. Ovoid body features evenly spaced vertical bands of three incised lines extending from neck to foot. Sits on ring foot.

Unpublished. Cf. for similar shape and decoration CVA Museo Nazionale Napoli 3 (Italy 24), pl. 64, no. 11, CVA Serres (France 13), Style Apulian, pl. 47, no. 8 and pl. 48, no. 6.

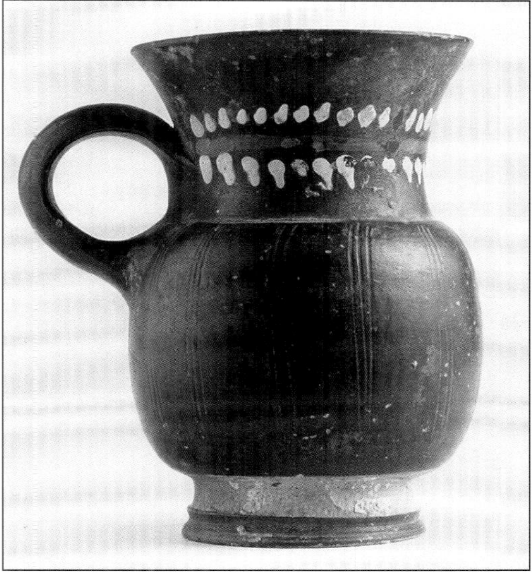

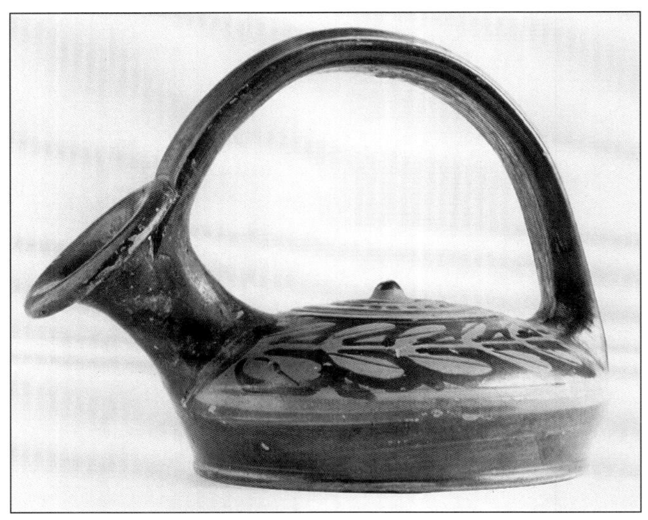

51
Apulian Askos
Ca. 350 B.C.
H. 4 1/2 in. 11.4 cm; w. 5 3/4 in. 14.6 cm
Transfer from UW Department of Classics, 70.18.2.
Purchased for teaching ancient art to classics students, probably in 1920s by Prof. Grant Showerman.

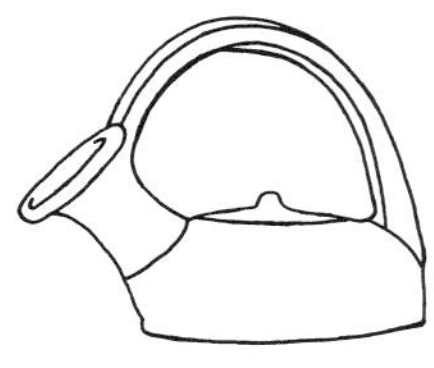

Condition: Intact. Many small areas of chipped and flaked paint throughout.

Decoration: Shiny black glaze on reddish earthenware. High, arching handle. Lid with knob handle, surrounded by radiating black lines. Rest of body dominated by red laurel-leaf motif in horizontal frieze.

Unpublished. For similar size and shape (without decoration), see Ann Steiner, *Joslyn Art Museum Ancient Greek Pottery* (Omaha, Neb. 1985), 80, pl. 35. Cf. CVA Sevres 1 (France 13), pl. 32, no. 12; CVA Museo Campano, Capua 3 (Italy 29), pl. 4, nos. 8,9.

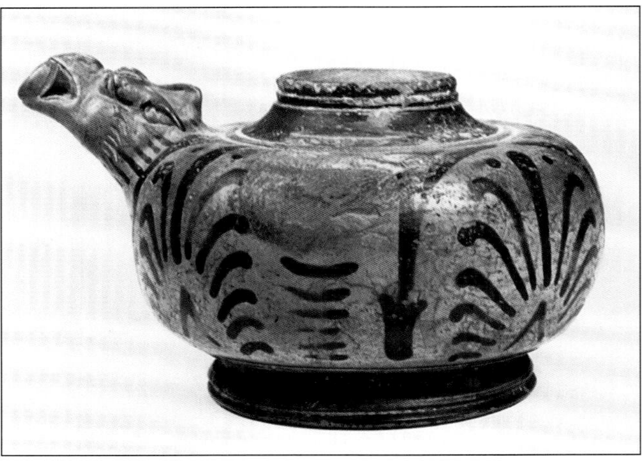

52
Apulian Askos
Ca. 350 B.C.
H. 3 1/2 in. 8.9 cm; w. 5 1/2 in. 14 cm
Transfer from UW Department of Classics, 70.18.4.
Purchased for teaching ancient art to classics students, probably in 1920s by Prof. Grant Showerman.

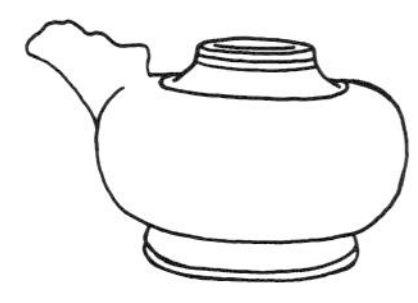

Condition: Intact. Soiled and abraded throughout; numerous scratches and tiny losses of pigment. Top rim and mouth displays heavy wear. Small gouges at rim. White debris accumulated in recessed details at animal head and at foot.

Decoration: Dark brown slip on orange body. Top of open-topped neck encircled by two incised lines. Neck and shoulder covered in dark brown slip. Two more incised lines with traces of white paint ring the askos where shoulder meets body. Beaked animal (griffin?) head spout with open mouth rises from upper body at approximately 45-degree angle. Plastic relief cheeks, eyes, and ears. Vertical dark brown bands from animal's throat to its neck. Orange body features six large palmettes in brown, separated by brown vegetation tendrils. Bottom of body has one thin line of brown beneath which is thicker band that spans area where body meets foot. Two small ridges around foot, all in brown. Sits on low ring foot. Inside low ring foot is bulls-eye pattern in brown with surrounding concentric circles in brown.

Unpublished. For similar animal spout, although slghtly different type of vase, see CVA Museo Campano, Capua 3 (Italy 29),ceramica interamente Verniciata, pl. 13, nos. 1–5.

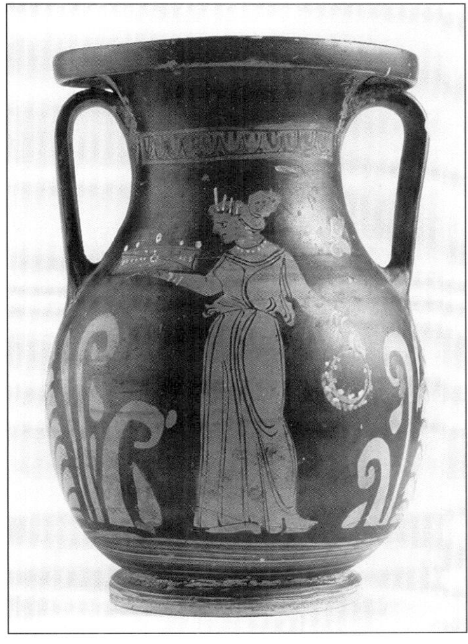

Side A

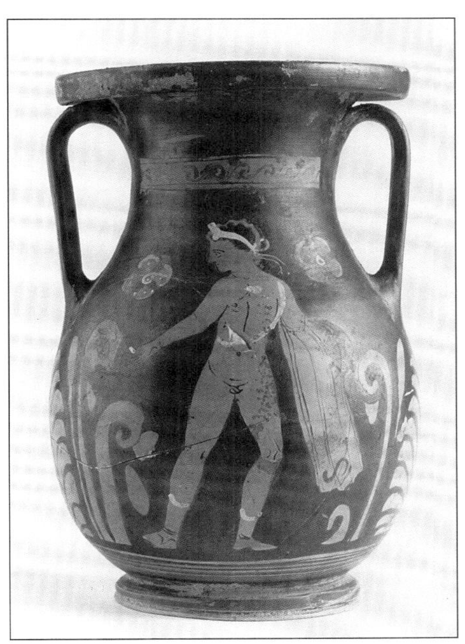

Side B

53
Apulian Red-figure Pelike
Close to the Waterspout Group (Attribution by A.D. Trendall)
Second–third quarter of 4th century B.C.
H. 6 3/4 in. 17.2 cm; d. rim 4 5/16 in. 10.9 cm; d. belly 4 7/16 in. 11.4 cm; d. foot 3 in. 7.6 cm
Transfer from UW Department of Classics, 70.18.8. Purchased for teaching ancient art to classics students, probably in 1920s by Prof. Grant Showerman.

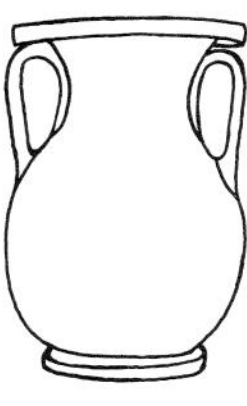

Condition: Reassembled. No repainting and seams of fragment edges jagged. Soiled and abraded throughout with scratches and residue at rim, interior, around handles, and top of foot.

Decoration: Palmettes beneath handles. On side A standing, draped woman with cista and wreath, above scene is band of egg-and-dot pattern; on side B nude youth with drapery over left arm moves to right, with border of wave-pattern band. White is added to wreath, prize, necklace, and spiked stephane of woman.

The Waterspout Group, according to Trendall, takes its name from the chous showing a woman collecting water in a phiale from a spout up above it. The vases noted as "close" to the Waterspout Group have similar treatment of women's drapery in the clearly defined fold-lines and drawing of leg beneath drapery.

Bibliography: Trendall and Cambitoglou, *The Red-Figured Vases of Apulia*, vol. 1, 293, no. 53a. Emilie Tari, "Some South Italian Vases in the Elvehjem Museum," M.A. Thesis University of Wisconsin, 1975, 52–55. Cf. CVA Museo de Antichità, Torino 1 (Italy 32), pl. 8, 1–2 and CVA Museo Provinciale, Lecce 4 (Italy 6), pl. 36, 13.

54
Apulian Bell Krater
Close to the Lucera Painter (Attribution by A. D. Trendall)
Ca. 340–320 B.C.
H. 11 in. 27.9 cm; d. rim 11 13/16 in. 29.9 cm; d. with handles 9 3/4 in. 24.8 cm; d. foot 5 1/4 in. 13.3 cm
Gift of Lucien M. Hanks, 68.13.1, lent to State Historical Society of Wisconsin 1922 by Mrs. L. M. Hanks, transferred to Elvehjem 1968, excavated from tomb at Lake Nemi, near Rome

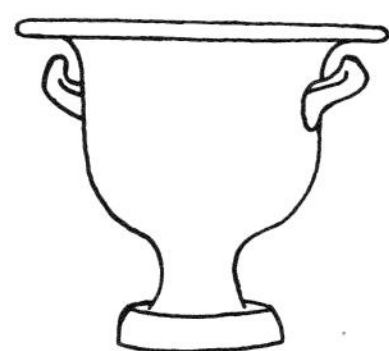

Condition: Intact. Heavily abraded. Patches of solidified residue on rim extending into interior and out along sides of exterior. Glaze heavily chipped and abraded at base of foot. Sharp linear indentations on circumference of belly.

Decoration: Reserved bands encircle the foot, the join of body and foot, and just below the band of reserved laurel leaves under the lip. Beneath the figural scene is a band of meanders and crossed squares. Beneath the handles are palmettes, and handles are encircled by black tongue pattern. On side A seated satyr with phiale, woman bending forward offering a bird in right hand and a bunch of grapes in left hand. On side B two youths face each other, each with a bare right shoulder and holding a staff. Between them hangs a pair of Halteres, or jumping weights,symbol of the palaestra.

Although Trendall tentatively attributed this vase in personal communication of 1968 to the Painter of the Truro Pelike; in his 1978 publication he does not list with Truro or even related vases but with vases connected in style to the Lucera Painter, who was a contemporary of the Painter of the Truro Pelike.

Bibliography: Trendall and Cambitoglou, *The Red-figured Vases of Apulia*, vol. 2, 579. Cf. Joslyn Art Museum 6.1984 by the group of the Painter of the Truro pelike, which has similar scenes on both sides: Steiner, *Joslyn Art Museum Ancient Greek Pottery*, 85, cat. no. 39.

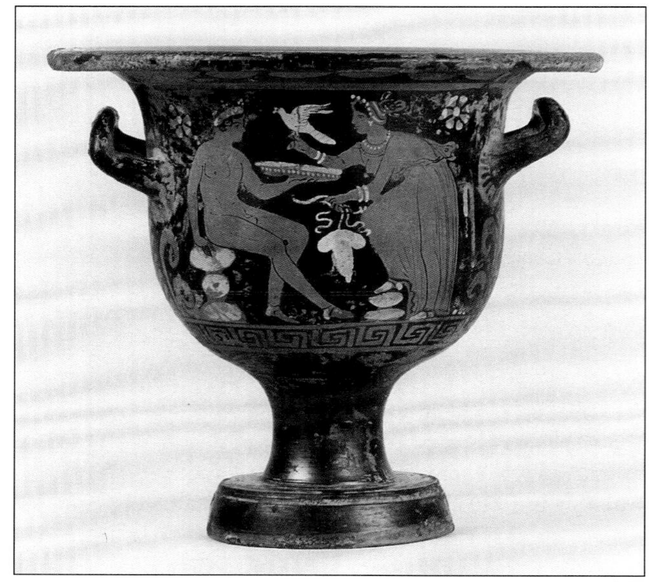

Side A

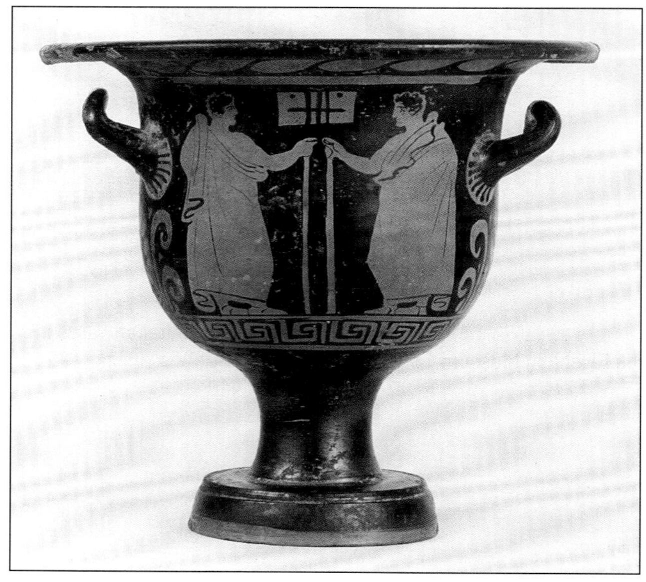

Side B

55
Apulian Kantharos
The Kantharos Group (Attribution by A.D. Trendall)
Last quarter of 4th century B.C.
H. 7 1/2 in. 19 cm; d. rim 4 7/16 in. 12.5 cm; d. with handles 7 1/8 in. 18.1 cm; d. without handles 4 3/8 in. 11.1 cm; d. foot 2 5/8 in. 6.7 cm
Transfer from UW Department of Classics, 70.18.9. Purchased for teaching ancient art to classics students, probably in 1920s by Prof. Grant Showerman.

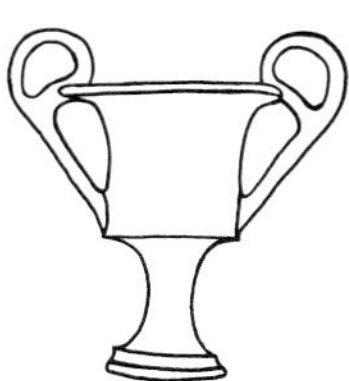

Condition: Intact. Small areas of chipped paint at sides of handles and interior of mouth.

Decoration: On each side is head of woman facing left, wearing elaborate sakkos and spiked sphendone. There is no vegetation, but sparing rosette fillers are used.

At least 500 vases decorated solely with female heads in profile to left are attributed to the Kantharos Group. The vases are mass products of a large workshop that employed several painters.

Bibliography: Trendall and Cambitoglou, *The Red-Figured Vases of Apulia*, vol. 2, 997, no. 427. Emilie Tari, "Some South Italian Vases in the Elvehjem Museum," M.A. Thesis University of Wisconsin, 1975, 55–60. Cf. CVA Fitzwilliam, Cambridge 1 (Great Britain 6), pl. 46, no.6.

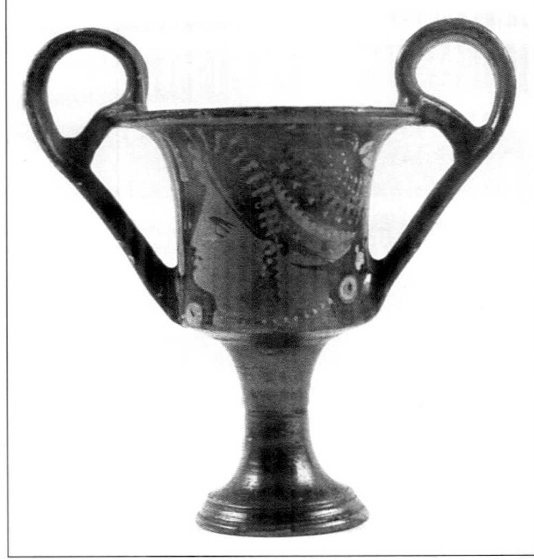

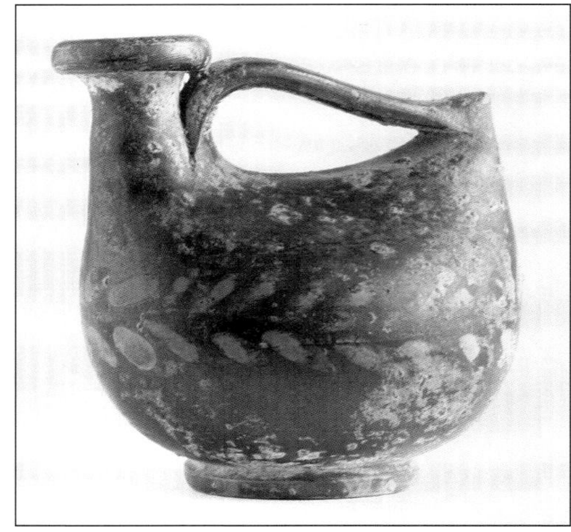

56
Apulian Gnathian Askos
4th century B.C.
H. 3 5/8 in. 9.2 cm; w. 4 in. 10.2 cm
Transfer from UW Department of Classics, 70.18.14. Purchased for teaching ancient art to classics students, probably in 1920s by Prof. Grant Showerman.

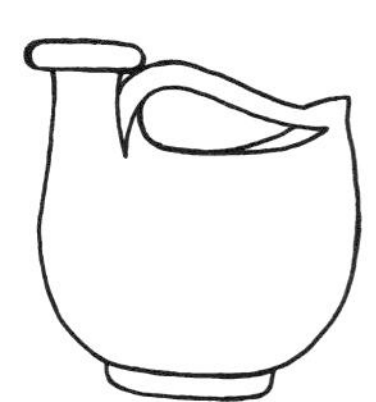

Condition: Intact. Heavily abraded and with debris concentrated at tips of handle and on belly of side B.

Decoration: Dull black glaze covers reddish earthenware. Vertical spout is thick, flaring. A continuous band of ivy leaves in red spans middle of body. It sits on a low ring foot.

Gnathia pottery, which was made in Apulia from around 370 to around 270 B.C., takes its name from ancient Gnathia (modern Egnazia) in Italy where vases of this type were first discovered in the mid-nineteenth century. It is now recognized that most vases of this type, which typically have designs in white, yellow, and red paint applied over black glaze, were made principally at Taranto.

Unpublished. Cf. CVA Museo Campano, Capua 3 (Italy 29), pl. 4, nos. 10, 11, 12; CVA Museo Nazionale, Napoli 3 (Italy 24), pl. 64, nos. 1,3,8; CVA National Museum, Copenhagen 7 (Danemark 7), pl. 280, no. 7.

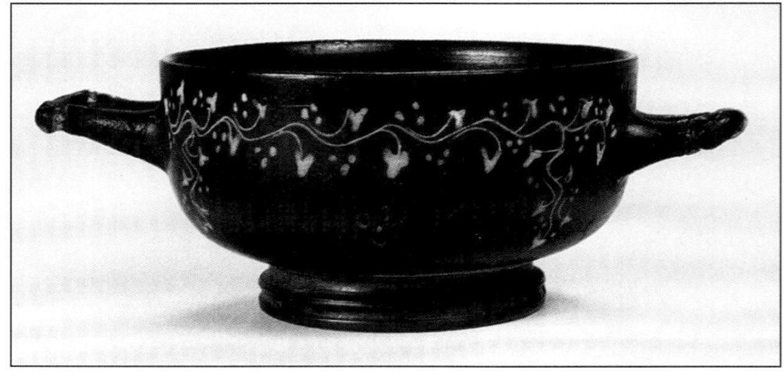

57
Apulian Gnathian Stemless Cup
4th century B.C.
H. 1 3/4 in. 4.5 cm; d. with handles 4 1/2 in. 11.4 cm; d. without handles 3 1/8 in. 7.9 cm; d. foot 1 7/8 in. 4.8 cm
Gift of Frances W. English, 1979.1145

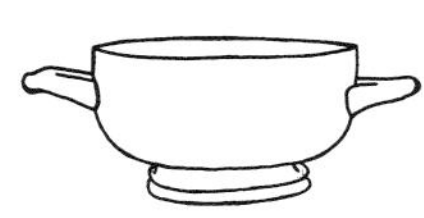

Condition: Top edge slightly chipped; two handles broken off and reattached, leaving thick yellow residue around seams.

Decoration: Under the lip is an ivy pattern with incised stems, white leaves, and grapes. Incised and painted decoration of grape vines.

Unpublished. Cf. Virginia Museum cups 91.52 and 81 in *The Art of South Italy: Vases from Magna Graecia*, cat. nos. 136 and 137; CVA Napoli Museo Nazionale 3 (Italy 24), pl. 63, no. 4.

58
Apulian Gnathian Squat Lekythos
Mid 4th century B.C.
H. 3 1/8 in. 8.9 cm; d. rim 1 1/8 in. 2.9 cm; d. belly 2 3/16 in. 5.6 cm; d. foot 1 1/2 in. 3.8 cm
Transfer from UW Department of Classics, 70.18.3.
Purchased for teaching ancient art to classics students, probably in 1920s by Prof. Grant Showerman.

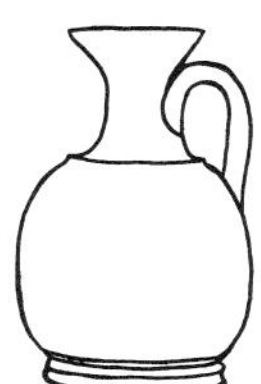

Condition: Intact. Small chip missing from outer rim; hairline crack from rim to neck. Abraded at rim, belly. No repainting.

Decoration: Thin black-glazed fabric with slightly flaring lip; thin neck with vertical loop handle. Ovoid body covered with impressed palmettes in slanted oval pattern; sits on low ring foot.

Unpublished. Cf. CVA Museo Campano, Capua 3 (Italy 29), pl. 7, no. 16; CVA National Museum, Copenhagen 7 (Danemark 7), pl. 287, nos. 4,8,9,10.

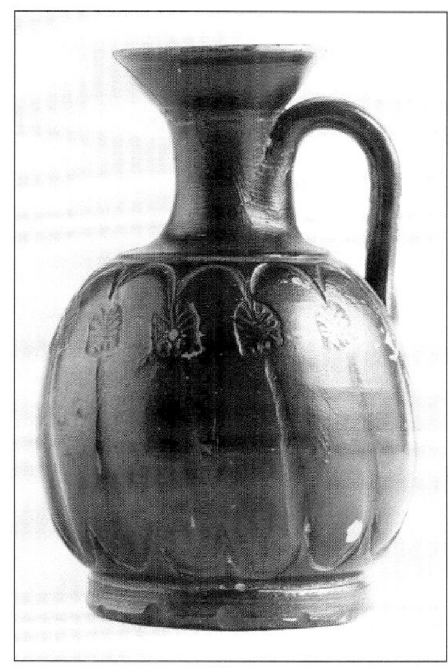

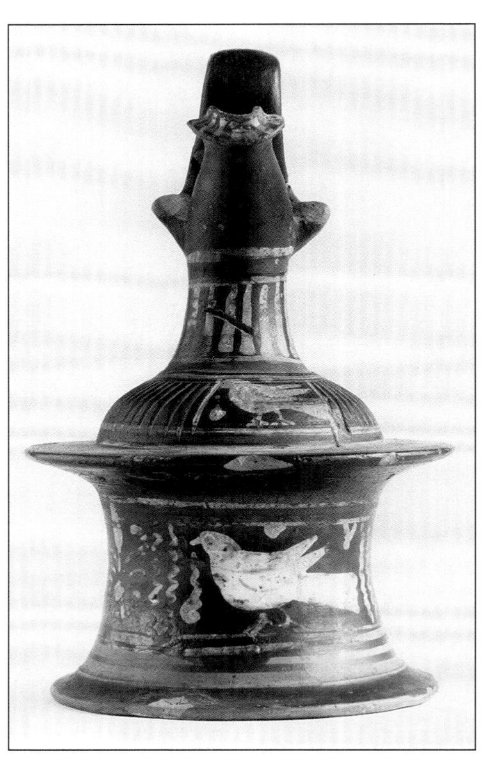

59
Apulian Gnathian Epichysis
Late 4th century B.C.
H. 6 3/8 in. 16.3 cm; d. rim 4 in. 10.2 cm; d. foot 3 5/8 in. 9.2 cm
Transfer from UW Department of Classics, 70.18.7.
Purchased for teaching ancient art to classics students, probably in 1920s by Prof. Grant Showerman.

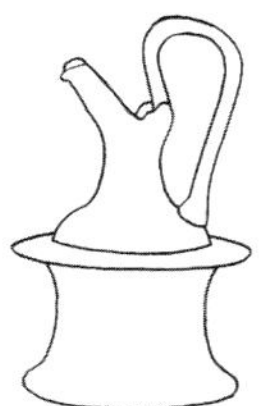

Condition: Intact with repairs to handle in which large fractures have been sealed at both ends and crack at top of handle. Chips, nicks around rim and boot. Gouge in neck.

Decoration: Orange earthenware with black glaze and added features in reddish purple, white, and yellow paint. The lip of the spout is decorated with vertical red bands. Two knobs painted red are formed at the join of the spout and angular high-swung strap handle. The neck is framed by horizontal band in red and white at top and bottom, which decorate three-quarters of the circumference, connected by vertical tongues running the length of the neck in white and yellow. The shoulder is framed at top and bottom by incised and painted lines, and incised lines painted over in white run vertically, interrupted by the handle join on one side. A bird facing left in white and yellow on the opposite side. An unidentifiable wavy figure hangs from the bird's mouth. The rim of the reel is decorated with concentric incised lines with white painted over and a band of red. An egg motif in white with added yellow runs inside the incised lines. The body of the reel is framed at top by horizontal concentric bands in white and red, and at bottom by reserved bands of orange. A bird (similar to the one on the shoulder), white with added features in yellow, faces left at the center, flanked by palmettes and vertical wavy lines in white and yellow.

Unpublished. For shape and color cf. CVA Baltimore, Robinson 3 (USA 7), Apulian: Gnathian, pl. 27, no. 2; CVA British Museum 1(Great Britain 1), Gnathia vases, pl. 6, nos. 20–23.

60
Apulian Gnathian Red-figure Epichysis
Ca. 350 B.C.
H. 6 1/2 in. 16.5 cm; d. 3 5/8 in. 9.2 cm
Gift in memory of Ellis E. Jensen, 1996.36

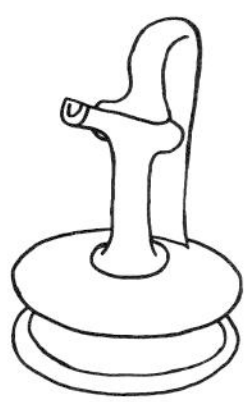

Condition: Reassembled with repaired fracture mid neck and mid handle; repainted at seam. Slight chipping of paint around projecting rim. White pigment abraded.

Decoration: Red-orange earthenware with black glaze has tongue pattern at neck; top of flange at shoulder is dominated by egg-and-dart pattern, while spokes encircle the join of neck and spout. The beaked spout is flanked at handle by two female heads in relief. On shoulder is naked youth, his left leg bent beneath him, the other stretched out behind him, both arms reach towards a bird. Youth is flanked by loose scrolls. Ivy leaves in added white decorate the body.

Bibliography: Elvehjem *Bulletin* (1995–97): 131 (illus.). Cf. CVA British Museum 1 (Great Britain 1): Italy and Sicily: Gnathia Vases, pl. 6, nos. 17, 21; CVA Museo Nazionale, Napoli 3 (Italy 24), pl. 71, nos. 3,5, pl. 72, no. 5; CVA Museo di Antichità, Torino 1 (Italy 32), pl. 18, no. 1.

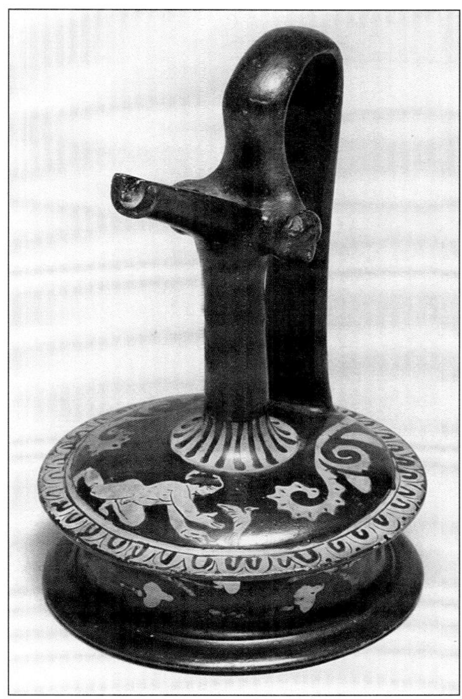

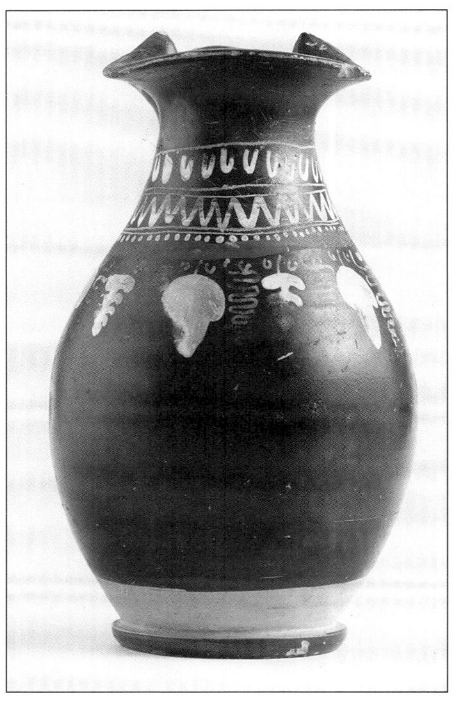

61
Apulian Gnathian Trefoil Oinochoe
Late 4th century B.C.
H. 5 3/4 in. 14.6 cm; d. 4 in. 10.2 cm
Transfer from UW Department of Classics, 70.18.11.
Purchased for teaching ancient art to classics students, probably in 1920s by Prof. Grant Showerman.

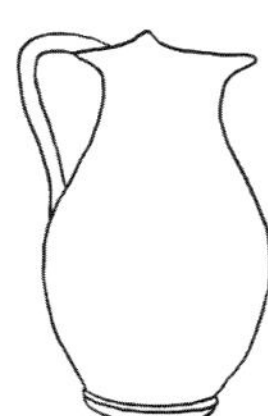

Condition: Intact but reassembled at left corner of rim. Chipped at rim and left side of handle; abraded and scratched throughout

Decoration: Thick black glazed earthenware fabric with trefoil mouth and low strap handle. Applied white, red, and yellow with reserved band of red around foot. Continuous line from mouth to foot. Painted decoration dominates upper neck to upper belly zone and is limited to front of oinochoe. Row of egg pattern in applied white with sloppily incised lines both above (one line) and below (two lines). Beneath egg pattern is a row of zigzag pattern in applied white with yellow brushed on top. This band is also defined by two incised lines beneath it. Line of deep red paint under incised lines on top of which were painted yellow-and-white dots. From a band of red paint hang five grape clusters in white with shading in yellow with white vine tendrils between each cluster.

Unpublished. For similar decoration cf. CVA British Museum 1 (Great Britain 1), Gnathia vases, pl. 5, no. 5; CVA Museo Nazionale, Napoli 3(Italy 24), pl. 65, nos. 4, 8; CVA Limoges and Vannes (France 24), Gnathia, pl. 33, no. 8 and bibliography of text that accompanies description.

62
Apulian Gnathian Squat Alabastron
Last half of 3rd century B.C.
H. 6 in. 15.2 cm; d. rim 2 1/8 in. 7.9 cm; d. of belly 3 in. 7.6 cm; d. foot 2 1/8 in. 5.4 cm
Transfer from UW Department of Classics, 70.18.15

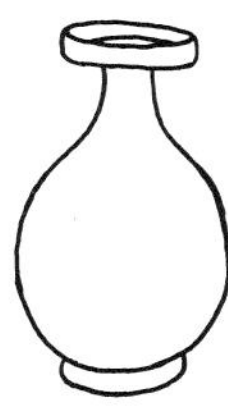

Condition: Intact. Crack on belly. Highly abraded with surface loss on rim and belly and paint cracked and flaking near decoration.

Decoration: Red-figure vase has decoration and detail in black, white, and yellow. Mouth and outer edge of lip is decorated with radiating black lines. A thick black band is around top of neck. Vertical black lines extend from neck to upper body with two black concentric circles above and one below. Side A is dominated by female head facing left, wearing kekryphalos with detail in white and yellow dots. Disks on either side of woman's head. White dots also emphasize woman's earrings and faded necklace. On side B a large palmette in black covers side. Vegetation tendrils in black flank palmette. Beneath heavily decorated zone is continuous black line around base of body. Foot is decorated in red and black bands. It sits on low ring foot.

Unpublished. For similar decoration, cf. CVA British Museum 1 (Great Britain 1), Gnathia Vases, pl. 4, no. 9. For similar shape, cf. CVA Museo Provinciale, Lecce 1 (Italy 4), Stile detto de Gnathia, pl. 6, no.5. For similar shape and decoration CVA Museo Nazionale, Napoli 3 (Italy 24), Gnathia, pl. 68, no. 14; CVA Limoges and Vannes (France 24), Gnathia, pl. 33, no.6.

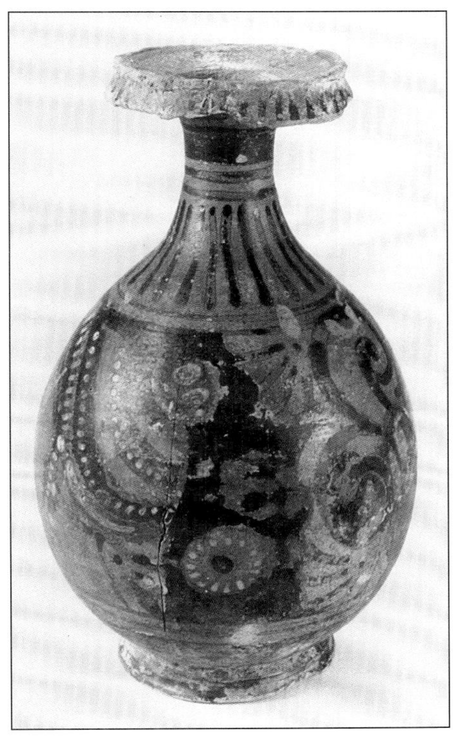

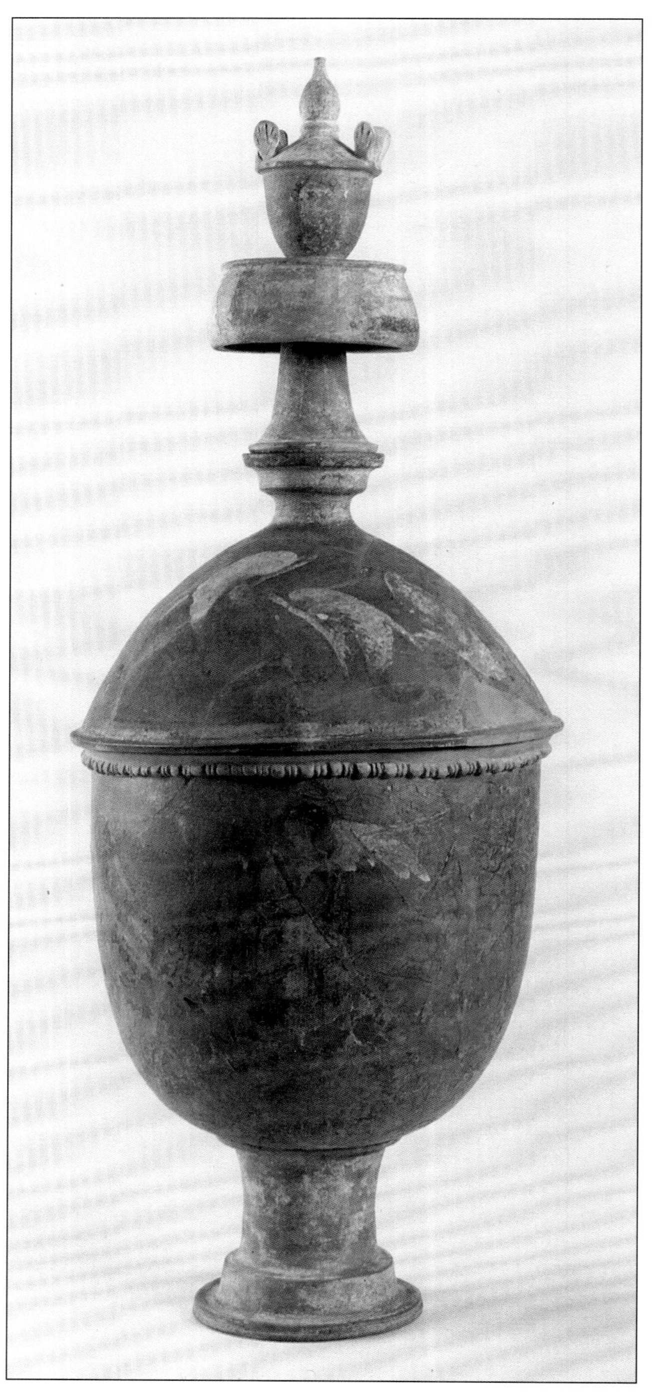

63
Sicilian (Centuripe) Domed Krater with Funerary Funnel
Ca. 300–100 B.C.
H. 28 in. 71 cm; d. 9 1/2 in. 24.1 cm; breaks down into five sections
Thomas E. Brittingham Fund purchase, 1976.28, Bruce McAlpine, Ltd., London; Salvestrini Collection, Switzerland

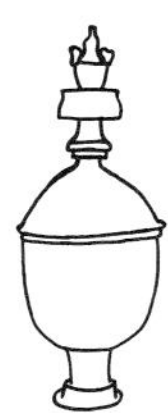

Condition: Cover is recomposed from seventeen fragments and missing triangular area at edge restored; the base is reassembled, the center of the painting of the main scene is obliterated.

Description: The urn is constructed in five pieces: pedestal base, domed lid, and three-part finial. It is painted in tempera pigments after firing in pastel tones of magenta, mauve, white, soft blue, and brown. The cover has five dolphins in dramatic poses, three toward the front and one on each side in different combinations of color such as blue body with brown snout and belly. There is no painting on the back of the lid or back of bowl. The shape of the finial duplicates the shape of the vase and has four palmette fans applied to the lid. The head of a woman is outlined in black and depicted in three-quarter view with soft, flowing hair and slender neck.

The main scene on the vase may refer to a wedding or some associated ritual. Nearly all detail is lost but on the left is a woman in profile facing right, with hands upraised and holding, perhaps, a distaff. She has long flowing hair, a necklace, and a himation with traces of blue. The center part of the picture is obliterated. A figure, or perhaps two, appears to be opening a chest, probably a wedding gift. Visible on a diagonal is an arm painted in flesh tones outlined in black. On the right is a seated winged figure, a Nike or victory figure. Her hair is tightly cropped, and the figure is in profile to the left. Her flesh is light orange-buff, her outer cloak is brown and blue, and her undergarment white. The short, furled wings are white and gray. The figures are painted with tonality and shading.

Bibliography: Christie's Antiquities Part 1 (July 10, 1974), Lot #4, illus. W. G. Moon, "An Enigmatic Vase from Centuripe," Elvehjem *Bulletin* (1975–76): n.p.

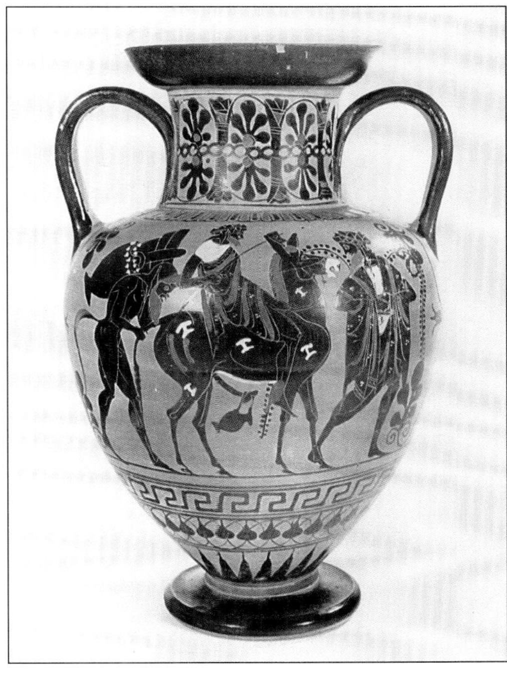

Side A

Attic Black-figure Neck-amphora
Painter from the Medea Group (Attribution by Deitrich von Bothmer)
Ca. 520 B.C.
H. 12 1/16 in. 30.9 cm; d. at shoulder 8 1/4 in. 21 cm; d. of mouth 5 in. 12.8 cm; d. foot 4 1/4 in. 10.7 cm
On extended loan from anonymous collection, 1.1978.1.
Purchased from Lincoln Higgie, Chicago

Condition: Intact and in excellent state of preservation, small chips and some scuffing.

Decoration: Side A shows return of Hephaestos in ivy wreath on ithyphallic donkey; side B has combat of Sythian and Amazon warriors with seconds.

Bibliography: Moon, *Greek Vase-Painting in Midwestern Collections*, 96–97, cat. no. 56.

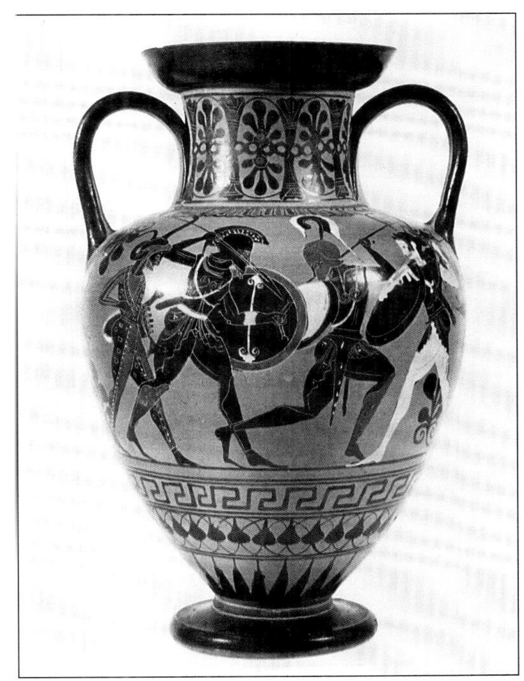

Side B

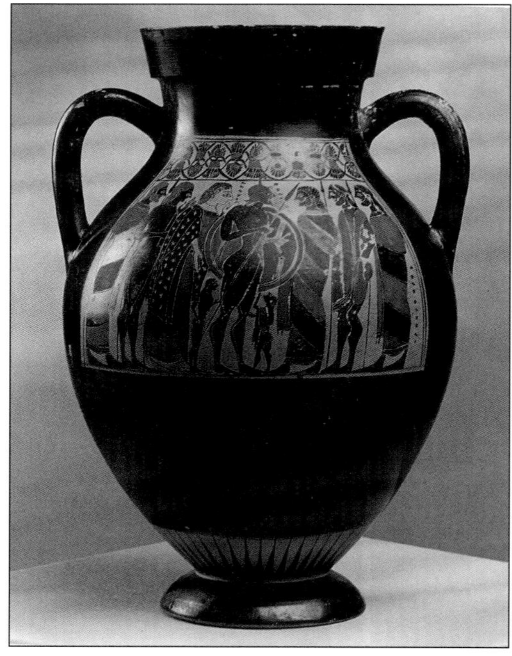

Side A

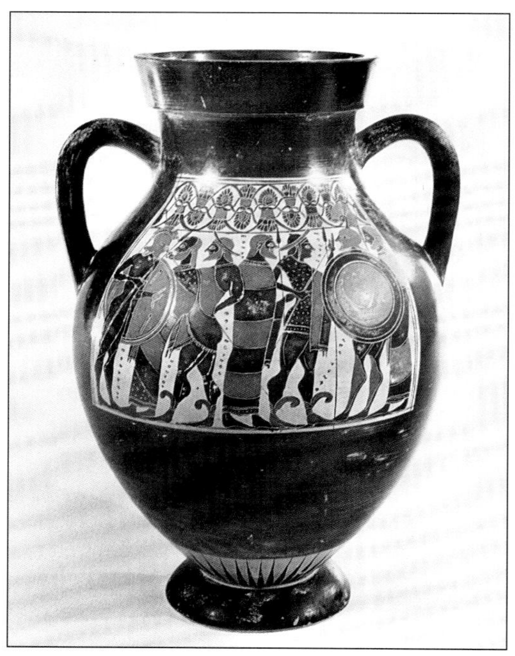

Side B

Black-figure Amphora (Type B)
The painter of Berlin 1686 (Attribution by Dietrich von Bothmer)
Ca. 550 B.C.
H. 11 1/2 in. 29.9 cm; w. 8 1/8 in. 20.6 cm; d. of mouth 4 15/16 in. 12.3 cm; d. foot 4 3/8 in. 10.6 cm
On extended loan from anonymous collection, 1.1978.2. Purchased from Lincoln Higgie, Chicago

Condition: Intact and in superior state of preservation. minor abrasion on handles, incrustation under foot and inside neck

Decoration: Side A shows warrior with long hair leaving home, carrying shield on left arm and spear in right; two children at feet and six other figures attend. Side B is assemblage of warriors and gods, including Hermes.

Bibliography: Moon, *Greek Vase-Painting in Midwestern Collections*, 56, cat. no. 32.

Works Cited in Catalogue

Amyx, D. A. *Corinthian Vase Painting of the Archaic Period*. Berkeley and Los Angeles 1980.

Amyx, D. A. "A Forged Corinthian Animal Frieze," Bulletin of the Brooklyn Museum 21.2 (1960), 9–13.

Beazley, J. D. *Attic Black-Figure Vase-Painters*. Oxford 1956. Abbreviation: ABV

Beazley, J. D. *Attic Red-Figure Vase-Painters*, 2nd ed.Oxford 1963. Abbreviation ARV2

Beazley, J. D. *Paralipomena: Additions to Attic Black-Figure Vase-Painters and to Attic Red-Figure Vase Painters*. Oxford 1971. Abbreviation: Para.

Benson, J. L. *Die Geschichte der Korinthischen Vasen*. Basel 1953, 47, pl. 9.

Biers, William. "Ancient Figure Vases in the Elvehjem," Elvehjem *Bulletin* (1987–88):12–17.

Cahn, H. *Art of the Ancients*. New York 1968.

Corpus Vasorum Antiquorum, various cities, various institutions, various dates. Abbreviation CVA

DePuma, Richard. *Etruscan and Villanovan Pottery*. Iowa City, Iowa 1971.

Del Chiaro, Mario. "An Early Etruscan Red Impasto Vase," Elvehjem *Bulletin* (1981–83): 29–31.

Eisman, M. M. "Attic Kyathos Production," *Archaeology* 28 (1975): 76–83.

Fairbanks, A. *Catalogue of Greek and Etruscan Vases*. Cambridge, Mass. 1928.

Gordon, Robert L. Jr., "Evidence for an Etruscan Workshop," *Muse* [Museum of Art and Archaeology, University of Missouri-Columbia] 5 (1971): 35–42.

Haldenstein, J. T. "Four Attic Black-figure Cups in the Elvehjem", Elvehjem *Bulletin* (1989–91): 6–12.

Havelock, Christine M. "Mourners on Greek Vases: Remarks on the Social History of Women." In *The Greek Vase* ed. Stephen L. Hyatt. Troy, N.Y. 1981. 115, pl. 93.

Kahane, P. P. "Ikonologische Untersuchungen zur griechischge-ometrischen Kunst: der Cesnola-Krater aus Kourion im Metropolitan Museum," *Antike Kunst* 16.2 (1973): 137, pl. 29.4.

Kahil, Lilly. *Lexicon Iconographicum Mythologiae Classicae*. Zurich 1984. 2: 695, no. 970, pl. 517.

Kurtz, D. C. *Athenian White Lekythoi: Patterns and Painters*. Oxford 1975. 27, 45, 206, pl. 25.3 and frontispiece.

Moon, W. G. "A Black-figure Neck-amphora by the Euphiletos Painter," Elvehjem *Bulletin* (1971–72): 8–15.

Moon, W. G. "An Enigmatic Vase from Centuripe," Elvehjem *Bulletin* (1975–76): n.p.

Moon, W. G. "A New Middle Corinthian Vase Painter in Madison: The Elvehjem Painter," *American Journal of Archaeology* 81 (1977): 382–89.

Moon, W. G. "The Priam Painter: Some Iconographic and Stylistic Considerations." In *Ancient Greek Art and Iconography* ed. W. G. Moon. Madison 1983.

Moon, W.G. "Two Vases in the Circle of the Antimenes Painter," Elvehjem Bulletin (1974–75): n.p.

Moon, W. G. and L. Berge. *Greek Vase-Painting in Midwestern Collections*. Chicago 1979.

Murlo and the Etruscans: Art and Society in Ancient Etruria, ed. Richard Daniel De Puma and Jocelyn Penny Small. Madison 1994.

Overby, Osmund, ed. *Illustrated Museum Handbook: A Guide to the Collections in the Museum of Art and Archaeology, University of Missouri-Columbia. Columbia*, 1982.

Steiner, Ann. Joslyn Art Museum Ancient Greek Pottery. Omaha, Neb. 1985.

Sweet, Harvey. "A Greek Lekythos and a Roman Season Sarcophagus in the Elvehjem Art Center," Ph.D. diss. University of Wisconsin–Madison, 1972.

Tari, Emilie. "Some South Italian Vases in the Elvehjem Museum," M.A. Thesis University of Wisconsin, 1975..

Thiersch, H. *Tyrrhenische Amphoren*. Leipzig 1899.

Trendall A.D. *The Red-Figured Vases of Lucania, Campania and Sicily*. Oxford 1967.

Trendall A. D. and Alexander Cambitoglou. *The Red-Figured Vases of Apulia. I. The Early and Middle Period. II. Late Apulian*. Oxford 1978.

Von Bothmer, D. "The Painters of 'Tyrrhenian' Vases, *American Journal of Archaeology* 48 (1944), 161–70.

Walter, Hans. *Griechishe Gotter*. Munich 1971. 203–4, fig. 180.

Virginia Museum of Fine Arts. *The Art of South Italy: Vases from Magna Graecia*. Richmond 1982. Abbreviation: The Art of South Italy.

Index